HARVARD CRIMSON MEN'S BASKETBALL PLAYERS

Table of Contents
Arne Duncan 1
Brian Cusworth 2
Cem Dinç 3
Eddie Grant (baseball) 3
Ed Smith (basketball) 5
James Brown (sportscaster) 5
Jeremy Lin 6
Keith Wright (basketball) 14
Lou Silver 14
Michael Crichton 15
Saul Mariaschin 24
Tony Lupien 24
Wyndol Gray 25

Preface
Each chapter in this book ends with a URL to a hyperlinked online version. Use the online version to access related pages, websites, footnotes, tables, color photos, updates, or to see the chapter's contributors. Click the edit link to suggest changes. Please type the URL exactly as it appears. If you change the URL's capitalization, for example, it may not work.

Purchase of this book entitles you to a free trial membership in the publisher's book club at www.booksllc.net. (Time limited offer.) Simply enter the barcode number from the back cover onto the membership form on our home page. The book club entitles you to select from millions of books at no additional charge, including a digital copy of this and related books to read on the go. Simply enter the title or subject onto the search form to find them.

If you have any questions, could you please be so kind as to consult our Frequently Asked Questions page at www.booksllc.net/faqs.cfm? You are also welcome to contact us there.

Publisher: Books LLC, Wiki Series, Memphis, TN, USA, 2012.

Arne Duncan

Arne Duncan

9th United States Secretary of Education
Incumbent
Assumed office
January 21, 2009
President   Barack Obama
Deputy   Anthony Miller
Preceded by   Margaret Spellings

Superintendent of Chicago Public Schools
In office
June 26, 2001 – January 21, 2009

Appointed by   Richard Daley
Preceded by   Paul Vallas
Succeeded by   Ron Huberman
Personal details
Born   November 6, 1964
Chicago, Illinois, United States
Political party   Democratic Party
Alma mater   Harvard University

Arne Duncan (born November 6, 1964) is an American education administrator and currently United States Secretary of Education. Duncan previously served as CEO of the Chicago Public Schools.

Early years and personal life

Duncan was raised in Hyde Park, a Chicago neighborhood encompassing the University of Chicago. He is the son of Susan Goodrich (née Morton) and Starkey Davis Duncan, Jr. His father was a psychology professor at the university and his mother runs the Sue Duncan Children's Center, an after-school program primarily serving African-American youth in the nearby Kenwood neighborhood. His ancestry includes Norwegian, Scottish, German, Swedish, and English; his maternal great-great-great-grandfather was U.S. Representative Milo Goodrich. While growing up, Duncan spent much of his free time at his mother's center tutoring or playing with students there. Some of his childhood friends were John W. Rogers, Jr., CEO of Ariel Capital Management (now Ariel Investments) and founder of the Ariel Community Academy, Illinois State Senator Kwame Raoul, actor Michael Clarke Duncan, singer R. Kelly and award winning martial artist Michelle Gordon.

Duncan after the 2012 State of the Union Address

Duncan attended the University of Chicago Laboratory Schools and later Harvard University, where he graduated magna cum laude in 1987 with a bachelor's degree in sociology. His senior thesis, for which he took a year's leave to do research in the Kenwood neighborhood, was entitled *The values, aspirations and opportunities of the urban underclass*.

While at Harvard, Duncan co-captained the varsity basketball team and was named a first team Academic All-American. From 1987 to 1991, Duncan played professional basketball, mostly in Australia, with teams including Melbourne's Eastside Spectres, of Australia's National Basketball League. Duncan also participated in the 2012 NBA All-Star Weekend Celebrity Game.

While in Australia, Duncan met his future wife, Karen Luann Duncan. They live in Arlington, Virginia. Their children, Claire and Ryan, attend public elementary school there.

In May 2012, he stated that he supports same-sex marriage.

Education career

Duncan at 2009 Obama Home States Inauguration Ball

In 1992, childhood friend and investment banker John W. Rogers, Jr. appointed Duncan director of the Ariel Education Initiative, a program mentoring children at one of the city's worst-performing elementary schools and then assisting them as they proceeded further in the education system. After the school closed in 1996, Duncan and Rogers were instrumental in re-opening it as a charter school, Ariel Community Academy. In 1999, Duncan was appointed Deputy Chief of Staff for former Chicago Public Schools CEO Paul Vallas.

Chicago public schools CEO

Mayor Richard M. Daley appointed Duncan to serve as Chief Executive Officer of the Chicago Public Schools on June 26, 2001. Opinions vary on Duncan's success as CEO; one prominent publication notes improved test scores and describes Duncan as a consensus builder, while another finds the improvements largely a myth and is troubled by the closing of neighborhood schools and their replacement by charter schools, and what it describes as schools' militarization.

Secretary of Education

Duncan was appointed U.S. Secretary of Education by President Barack Obama and confirmed by the Senate on January 20, 2009. One of Duncan's well-known initiatives as secretary has been a $4 billion Race to the Top competition. It asks states to vie for federal education dollars by submitting proposals that include reforms such as expanding charter schools and judging teachers partly on how well their students do on standardized tests. Duncan sends his own children to public schools. In March 2011 Duncan said 82 percent of the nation's public schools could be failing by next year under the standards of the No Child Left Behind law. The projection amounts to a startling spike from current data, which shows that 37 percent of schools are on track to miss targets set by the law. He said "Four out of five schools in America would not meet their goals under [No Child Left Behind] by next year," Duncan said in his opening statement. "This is why we have to fix the law now. Nobody can support inaction and maintain the status quo."

Criticism

Teachers' unions, such as the National Education Association (NEA), have criticized the Obama Administration's embrace of charter schools as part of the Race to the Top. The NEA gave the Race to the Top a vote of "no confidence," and invited critic Diane Ravitch to speak at their 2010 meeting. In February 2012, Duncan was criticized for appearing publicly on a panel with Michelle Rhee—former Washington D. C. Chancellor of Schools. The Office of the Inspector General of the Department of Education (the Department which Duncan heads) was, at that time, investigating whether D.C. schools had cheated to raise test scores during Rhee's tenure. On February 26, 2012, the New York Times quoted criticisms of Duncan by Richard L. Hyde, an investigator who exposed the large-scale test-score cheating that was endemic in Atlanta (Georgia) City Schools: "'I'm shocked that the secretary of education would be fraternizing with someone who could potentially be the target of the investigation,' [Hyde] said. 'The appearance of a conflict of interest is troubling because it can cause the public to lose faith in the investigation.'"

Source http://en.wikipedia.org/wiki/Arne_Duncan

Brian Cusworth

Maine Red Claws		**Born**	March 9, 1984	**High school**	John Burroughs HS (Ladue, Missouri)
Center			St. Louis, Missouri, USA		
Personal information				**Listed height**	7 ft 0 in (2.13 m)
		Nationality	American		

Listed weight	255 lb (116 kg)
Career information	
College	Harvard (2002–2007)
NBA Draft	2007 / Undrafted
Pro career	2007–present
League	NBA D-League

Career history
Tartu Ülikool/Rock (2007–2008)
CB Breogán (2008–2009)
Bàsquet Manresa (2009–2010)
Maine Red Claws (2012–present)

Career highlights and awards
KML Most Valuable Player 2008
KML Finals MVP 2008

Brian Cusworth (born March 9, 1984) is an American professional basketball player.

Brian Cusworth started playing basketball at the age of nine in 1993 in his hometown St. Louis. After graduating high school he went to study at Harvard University and played NCAA basketball at Harvard Crimson team for three seasons. In 2007 he went to play in Europe and signed a deal with Estonian top team Tartu Ülikool/Rock. He was one of the team's top performers during the season and helped Rock to FIBA EuroCup semifinals. He also won the Estonian National Championship with the team.

On November 1, 2012, Cusworth signed with the Maine Red Claws.

Achievements
Estonian National Championship 2007–08
Estonian League Most Valuable Player 2007-08
Estonian League Finals MVP 2007–08
Estonian Basketball Cup runner-up 2007–08
FIBA EuroCup runner-up 2007-08
Source http://en.wikipedia.org/wiki/Brian_Cusworth

Cem Dinç

Pınar Karşıyaka
PF/SF (Frontcourt)

Personal information
Born	July 23, 1985 Bassum, Germany
Nationality	Turkey-Germany
Listed height	6 ft 11 in (2.11 m)
Listed weight	245 lb (111 kg)
Career information	
Pro career	2005–present
League	Turkish League

Career history
UBC Münster (Germany)
Indiana Hoosiers (NCAA)

Cem Dinç (born July 23, 1985 in Bassum, Germany) is a Turkish-German basketball player in the Frontcourt Positions who plays for Pınar Karşıyaka in Turkey.

Early life

Cem was born into a family of Turkish father Ismail Cem Dinç and German mother Ingrid Dinç, growing up in Germany has a brother, Dirk. His father, a medical doctor, was a former national champion and world-class track star in the 110 m hurdles. His father helped him work on his strength, speed, and agility by focusing on sprints and plyometrics. This increased his explosiveness and jumping ability, making him an excellent athlete for a player of his size. Cem runs the 100 m in 10.8 seconds.

Career in Germany

Cem played high school basketball at Landschulheim Schloss Heessen in Hamm, Germany.

After receiving limited playing time in Germany and the German 2. Bundesliga, Cem moved to the United States, signing with the Indiana Hoosiers at Indiana University.
2002-04 UBC Münster - Bundesliga 2
2003-04 Iserlohn Roosters - Bundesliga 2

NCAA

In his first NCAA season in 2005-06, he played for the Indiana Hoosiers at Indiana University in Bloomington, Indiana, U.S.. He transferred to Marshalltown Community College for NJCAA in Iowa, U.S., for the 2006-07 season. After graduating from Marshalltown Community College, Cem enrolled at Harvard University in the fall of 2007, being expected to graduate with an A.B. in Economics as a member of the class of 2010.
2005-06 Indiana Hoosiers - NCAA
2006-07 Marshalltown CC - NJCAA
2007-08 Harvard Crimson - NCAA
2008-09 Harvard Crimson - NCAA

Career in Turkey

On 9 January 2010, Turkish Basketball League team Pınar Karşıyaka transferred him from Hacettepe University. At Hacettepe he averaged 4.5 points in 8 games.
2009-10 Hacettepe University - TB2L
2009-10 Pınar Karşıyaka - TBL

National squad

Cem Dinç was discovered for the Turkish National squad after he graduated from high school in 2005. He was named to the Turkish squad for the World Basketball Championship in 2006, Japan.

Source http://en.wikipedia.org/wiki/Cem_Dinç

Eddie Grant (baseball)

Eddie Grant

Eddie Grant (baseball)

Infielder

Born: May 21, 1883
Franklin, Massachusetts

Died: October 5, 1918 (aged 35)
Argonne Forest, France

Batted: Left   **Threw:** Right

MLB debut
August 4, 1905 for the Cleveland Naps

Last MLB appearance
October 6, 1915 for the New York Giants

Career statistics

Batting average	.249
Hits	844
RBI	277
Stolen bases	153

Teams

Cleveland Naps (1905)
Philadelphia Phillies (1907-1910)
Cincinnati Reds (1911-1913)
New York Giants (1913-1915)

Edward Leslie Grant (May 21, 1883 – October 5, 1918), was an American third baseman in Major League Baseball who became one of the few major leaguers who were killed in World War I.

Biography

He was born on May 21, 1883 in Franklin, Massachusetts.

After completing high school in 1901, Grant attended Dean Academy (now Dean College) in Franklin for a year before enrolling at Harvard University (earning him the nickname "Harvard Eddie"). While at Harvard, Grant was a member of the freshman basketball and baseball teams. He played varsity basketball for the Crimson during his sophomore year in 1903, and was set to play varsity baseball the following spring until he was declared ineligible for playing in a professional independent baseball league the previous summer. He graduated from Harvard University with an undergraduate degree in 1905 and a law degree in 1909.

Grant entered the majors with the Cleveland Indians at the very end of the 1905 season as an emergency replacement for an ailing Nap Lajoie. He played in the minor leagues in 1906, but returned to the majors with the Philadelphia Phillies in 1907, and was the Phillies' starting third baseman from 1908-1910. Grant batted leadoff for the Phillies, but was known more for his fielding and base stealing than his bat. His best year was 1910, when he batted .268, drove in 67 runs, and stole 25 bases.

Traded to the Cincinnati Reds in 1911, he batted just .223, his last year as a starter. Grant was traded again to the New York Giants in the middle of the 1913 season, where he finished his career as a utility infielder. Grant appeared in two games of the 1913 World Series, once as a pinch runner and once as a pinch hitter. He retired after the 1915 season. His lifetime batting average was .249.

Eddie Grant as Captain during WWI

Post-career

Upon his retirement from baseball, he opened a law practice in Boston.

Grant was one of the first men to enlist when the United States entered World War I in April 1917, and he served as a Captain in the 77th Infantry Division. During the fierce battle of the Meuse-Argonne Offensive, all of Grant's superior officers were killed or wounded, and he took command of his troops on a four-day search for the "Lost Battalion." During the search, an exploding shell killed Grant on October 5, 1918. He was the first Major League Baseball player killed in action in World War I. He was buried at the Meuse-Argonne American Cemetery in Lorraine, France.

Legacy

On Memorial Day, May 29, 1921, representatives from the armed forces, baseball, and the sisters of Grant unveiled a monument in center field of the Polo Grounds to his memory. During the celebration at the end of the last Giants' game in 1957, someone pried the plaque from its monument. It was missing for over 40 years until it was claimed re-discovered in a Ho-Ho-Kus, New Jersey home that had been owned by a New York City police officer. However, the photo shown of the supposed plaque on the Internet does not look like the missing plaque from the Polo Grounds, which has now been replicated at the San Francisco Giants current ballpark as of 2006.

Grant is also memorialized with the Edward L. Grant Highway in The Bronx, New York and by Grant Field at Dean College.

Source http://en.wikipedia.org/wiki/Eddie_Grant_(baseball)

Ed Smith (basketball)

No. 14
Forward
Personal information
Born July 5, 1929
West Jefferson, Ohio
Nationality American
Died November 25, 1998
(aged 69)
Listed height 6 ft 6 in (1.98 m)
Listed weight 180 lb (82 kg)
Career information
College Harvard
NBA Draft 1951 / Round: 1 / Pick: 6th overall
Selected by the New York Knicks
Pro career 1953–1954
Career history
1953–1954 New York Knicks

Edward "Ed" Smith (July 5, 1929 - November 25, 1998) was an NBA basketball player for the New York Knicks. He was drafted with the sixth pick in the first round of the 1951 NBA Draft by the Knicks. He made his NBA debut in the 1953-54 NBA season and played in eleven games where he averaged 2.5 points per game and 2.4 rebounds per game.

Source http://en.wikipedia.org/wiki/Ed_Smith_(basketball)

James Brown (sportscaster)

James Brown
Born February 25, 1951
Washington, D.C., U.S.
Occupation Sportscaster
Spouse(s) Dorothy
Children Katrina

James Brown (born February 25, 1951), commonly called "J.B.", is an American sports announcer known for being the host of *The NFL Today* on CBS and *Inside the NFL* on Showtime. He is the former host of the FOX network's NFL pregame show, *Fox NFL Sunday*.

Early life

Born on February 25, 1951 in Washington, D.C. to John and Maryann Brown. Brown attended high school at DeMatha Catholic High School. Brown graduated from Harvard University with a degree in American Government. A standout on the basketball court, he received All-Ivy League honors in his last three seasons at Harvard University and captained the team in his senior year. His roommate at Harvard was the later Princeton University professor/philosopher/activist Cornel West.

CBS

After failing to make a roster spot when he tried out for the NBA's Atlanta Hawks in the mid 1970s, Brown entered the corporate world, working for such companies as Xerox and Eastman Kodak. Brown went into sports broadcasting in 1984 when he was offered a job doing Washington Bullets television broadcasts. He later moved on to an anchor position at WDVM-TV (later WUSA) in Washington and to some work at CBS Sports. Brown first joined CBS Sports in 1984 where he served as play-by-play announcer for the network's NFL and college basketball coverage, as well as reporter for the NBA Finals. He also was host of the afternoon show from the 1992 Winter Olympics in Albertville, France and the 1994 Winter Olympics in Lillehammer, Norway. While at CBS he also was co-host of *CBS Sports Saturday/Sunday*, a weekend anthology series.

FOX, and back to CBS

In 1994, Brown accepted the position of host of the *NFL on Fox* pregame show. He shared the set with former football players Terry Bradshaw and Howie Long and former coach Jimmy Johnson. Cris Collinsworth and Ronnie Lott have also appeared on the program during Brown's time there.

From 1994–1998, Brown was the lead studio host for *FOX NHL Saturday*. He appeared in a similar capacity in the EA Sports video game *NHL '97*, which used full-motion video. His voice appeared in Madden NFL 2001.

Following the 2005 NFL season, Brown left Fox in order to rejoin CBS Sports. Brown cited a desire to remain closer to his home in Washington D C, an opportunity that existed at CBS, which broadcasts *The NFL Today* out of New York City. *Fox NFL Sunday* is produced in Los Angeles.

Brown was removed from college basketball coverage for CBS after a one year stint in 2007.

Brown also primary hosts the college basketball pregame, halftime and postgame in the CBS studios in New York City Greg Gumbel is the main host but sometimes Brown fills in when Gumbel is on a another assignment.

Other appearances

Brown has also hosted *The World's Funniest!* (the Fox network's counterpart of *America's Funniest Home Videos*), *Coast to Coast* (a syndicated radio show formerly hosted by Bob Costas), and served as a correspondent for *Real Sports with Bryant Gumbel*. Brown appeared on an episode of *Married...with Children* in a November 24, 1996 episode titled "A Bundy Thanksgiving".

Aside from his Showtime and CBS duties, Brown hosted a weekday radio sports talk show that aired weekdays on Sporting News Radio for several years. Brown left the network in April 2006. He has since, returned to Sporting News Radio with Arnie Spanier.

Brown regularly appeared on the syndicated radio program, *The Don and Mike Show*.

In March 2009, James Brown was

named the Community Ambassador for AARP.

On Aug. 10, 2009, Brown interviewed NFL quarterback Michael Vick for a segment that aired on *60 Minutes* Aug. 16.

Career timeline
1985–1986: *College Basketball on CBS* - Color Commentator
1990–1993, 2007: *College Basketball on CBS* - Play-by-play
1994–2006: *Fox NFL Sunday* - Host
1994–1998: *NHL on Fox* - Studio host
2006–present: *The NFL Today* - Host
2008–present: *Inside the NFL* - Host

Personal life
Brown resides outside of Washington, D.C. in Bethesda, MD, his town of birth, with his wife Dorothy and daughter Katrina. He formerly had a second residence in Century City, California, when working on FOX as their NFL program was based in Los Angeles. He was also named one of the 100 most influential student athletes by the NCAA. He has three granddaughters, born to his daughter, Katrina and her husband John.

On May 3, 2006, Brown became a minority owner of the Washington Nationals Major League Baseball team. Brown was one of a handful of investors in the group led by Washington, D.C. real estate developer Ted Lerner.

Source http://en.wikipedia.org/wiki/James_Brown_(sportscaster)

Jeremy Lin

Jeremy Lin at the 2012 Time 100 Gala.

No. 7 – Houston Rockets
Point guard

Personal information
Born	August 23, 1988 Los Angeles, California
Nationality	American
High school	Palo Alto HS (Palo Alto, California)
Listed height	6 ft 3 in (1.91 m)
Listed weight	200 lb (91 kg)

Career information
College	Harvard (2006–2010)
NBA Draft	2010 / Undrafted
Pro career	2010–present

Career history
2010–2011	Golden State Warriors
2010–2011	→Reno Bighorns (D-League)
2011	Dongguan Leopards (China)
2011–2012	New York Knicks
2012	→Erie BayHawks (D-League)
2012–present	Houston Rockets

Career highlights and awards
NBA Rising Star (2012)
ABA Club Championship MVP (2011)
2× All-Ivy League First Team (2009, 2010)
All-Ivy League Second Team (2008)
CIF Division II champion (2006)
2× SCVAL MVP (2005, 2006)
Stats at NBA.com
Stats at Basketball-Reference.com

Jeremy Lin
Traditional Chinese 林書豪
Simplified Chinese 林书豪

Jeremy Shu-How Lin (born August 23, 1988) is an American professional basketball player for the Houston Rockets of the National Basketball Association (NBA).

After receiving no athletic scholarship offers out of high school and being undrafted out of Harvard University, Lin reached a partially guaranteed contract deal in 2010 with his hometown Golden State Warriors. He seldom played in his rookie season and was assigned to the NBA Development League (D-League) three times. He was waived by the Warriors and the Rockets the following preseason before joining the New York Knicks early in the 2011–12 season. He continued to play sparingly and again spent time in the D-League. In February 2012, he unexpectedly led a winning streak by New York while being promoted to the starting lineup, which generated a global following known as *Linsanity*. In the summer of 2012, Lin signed a three-year contract with the Rockets.

Lin is one of the few Asian Americans in NBA history, and the first American of Chinese or Taiwanese descent to play in the league. He is also known for his public expression of his Christianity.

Early life
Lin was born in Los Angeles, and raised in a Christian family in the San Francisco Bay Area city of Palo Alto. His parents, Lin Gie-Ming and Shirley Lin, emigrated from Taiwan to the United States in the mid-1970s, settling first in Virginia before moving to Indiana, where they both attended universities. They are dual nationals of both Taiwan and the U.S. Lin's paternal family comes from Beidou, Changhua, in Taiwan (his father's distant ancestors were from Zhangpu County, Fujian, in mainland China, and settled in Taiwan in 1707), while his maternal grandmother emigrated to Southern Taiwan in the late 1940s from Pinghu, Zhejiang in mainland China.

Lin's parents are both 5 feet 6 inches (1.68 m) tall. His maternal grandmother's family was tall, and her father was over 6 feet (1.8 m). Lin has an older brother, Josh, and a younger brother, Joseph. Gie-Ming taught his sons to play basketball at the local YMCA. Shirley helped form a National Junior Basketball program in Palo Alto where Lin played. She worked with coaches to ensure his playing did not affect academics. She was criticized by her friends for letting Lin play so much basketball, but she allowed him to play the game he enjoyed.

High school career

In his senior year in 2005–2006, Lin captained Palo Alto High School to a 32–1 record and upset nationally ranked Mater Dei, 51–47, for the California Interscholastic Federation (CIF) Division II state title. He was named first-team All-State and Northern California Division II Player of the Year, ending his senior year averaging 15.1 points, 7.1 assists, 6.2 rebounds and 5.0 steals.

College career

Recruiting process

Lin sent his résumé and a DVD of highlights of his high-school basketball career to all the Ivy League schools, University of California, Berkeley, and his dream schools Stanford and University of California, Los Angeles (UCLA). The Pac-10 schools wanted him to walk-on, rather than be actively recruited or offered a sports scholarship. Harvard and Brown were the only teams that guaranteed him a spot on their basketball teams, but Ivy League schools do not offer athletic scholarships. Rex Walters, University of San Francisco men's basketball coach and a retired NBA player, said NCAA limits on coaches' recruiting visits had an impact on Lin's chances. "Most colleges start recruiting a guy in the first five minutes they see him because he runs really fast, jumps really high, does the quick, easy thing to evaluate," Walters said. Lin added, "I just think in order for someone to understand my game, they have to watch me more than once, because I'm not going to do anything that's extra flashy or freakishly athletic."

In July 2005, then-Harvard assistant coach Bill Holden saw that Lin was 6 feet 3 inches (1.91 m), which fitted the physical attributes he was seeking, and he had a 4.2 grade point average in high school, which fitted Harvard's academic standards. But Holden was initially unimpressed with Lin's on-court abilities, and told Lin's high school basketball coach, Peter Diepenbrock, that Lin was a "Division III player". Later that week, Holden saw Lin playing in a much more competitive game, driving to the basket at every opportunity with the "instincts of a killer", and Lin became a top priority for him. Harvard coaches feared that Stanford, close to Lin's home, would offer Lin a scholarship, but it did not, and Lin chose to attend Harvard. "I wasn't sitting there saying all these Division I coaches were knuckleheads," Diepenbrock said. "There were legitimate questions about Jeremy." Joe Lacob, incoming Warriors' owner and Stanford booster, said Stanford's failure to recruit Lin "was really stupid. The kid was right across the street. [If] you can't recognize that, you've got a problem." Kerry Keating, the UCLA assistant who offered Lin the opportunity to walk-on, said in hindsight that Lin would probably have ended up starting at point guard for UCLA.

Harvard

A Harvard coach remembered Lin in his freshman season as "the [physically] weakest guy on the team", but in his sophomore season (2007–08), Lin averaged 12.6 points and was named All-Ivy League Second Team. By his junior year during the 2008–09 season, he was the only NCAA Division I men's basketball player who ranked in the top ten in his conference for scoring (17.8), rebounding (5.5), assists (4.3), steals (2.4), blocked shots (0.6), field goal percentage (0.502), free throw percentage (0.744), and three-point shot percentage (0.400), and was a consensus selection for All-Ivy League First Team. He had 27 points, 8 assists, and 6 rebounds in an 82–70 win over 17th-ranked Boston College, three days after the Eagles defeated No. 1 North Carolina.

In his senior year (2009–10), Lin averaged 16.4 points, 4.4 rebounds, 4.5 assists, 2.4 steals and 1.1 blocks, and was again a unanimous selection for All-Ivy League First Team. He was one of 30 midseason candidates for the John R. Wooden Award and one of 11 finalists for the Bob Cousy Award. He was also invited to the Portsmouth Invitational Tournament. Fran Fraschilla of ESPN picked Lin among the 12 most versatile players in college basketball. He gained national attention for his performance against the 12th-ranked Connecticut Huskies, against whom he scored a career-high tying 30 points and grabbed 9 rebounds on the road. After the game, Hall of Fame Connecticut coach Jim Calhoun said of Lin: "I've seen a lot of teams come through here, and he could play for any of them. He's got great, great composure on the court. He knows how to play."

For the season, Harvard set numerous

After failing to receive any athletic scholarship offers, Lin attended Harvard.

program records including wins (21), non-conference wins (11), home wins (11) and road/neutral wins (10). Lin finished his career as the first player in the history of the Ivy League to record at least 1,450 points (1,483), 450 rebounds (487), 400 assists (406) and 200 steals (225). He graduated from Harvard in 2010 with a degree in economics and a 3.1 grade-point average.

Professional career

Undrafted

At the Portsmouth Invitational, Lin first met sports agent Roger Montgomery and later gave him a commitment. To their disappointment, no team chose Lin in the 2010 NBA Draft. The NBA had not drafted an Ivy League player since Jerome Allen of Penn in the second round in 1995. The last Ivy League player to play in the NBA was Yale's Chris Dudley in 2003, while the last Harvard player was Ed Smith in 1954. Eight teams had invited Lin to predraft workouts. Diepenbrock said that NBA tryouts do not play five on five. Lin acknowledged that the workouts were "one on one or two on two or three on three, and that's not where I excel. I've never played basketball like that." Scouts saw what *The New York Times* later described as "a smart passer with a flawed jump shot and a thin frame, who might not have the strength and athleticism to defend, create his own shot or finish at the rim in the N.B.A." Lin joined the Dallas Mavericks for minicamp as well as their NBA Summer League team in Las Vegas. Donnie Nelson of the Mavericks was the only General Manager who offered him an invitation to play in the Summer League. "Donnie took care of me," said Lin. "He has a different type of vision than most people do."

In five Summer League games, while playing both guard positions, Lin averaged 9.8 points, 3.2 rebounds, 1.8 assists, and 1.2 steals in 18.6 minutes per game and shot a team leading 54.5% from the floor. He outplayed first overall pick John Wall; Lin scored 13 points to Wall's 21, but did so on 6-for-12 shooting in 28 minutes. Wall was 4-for-19 in 33 minutes. While Wall received the biggest cheer for any player during introductions, the crowd turned on Wall and was cheering for Lin by the end of the game. Lin was reluctant to play overseas without an NBA offer and only planned to do so for a year before finding a non basketball-related job, but after the summer league received offers from the Mavericks, Los Angeles Lakers, Golden State Warriors, and an unnamed Eastern Conference team.

Golden State Warriors (2010–2011)

Lin at Warriors practice in 2010

On July 21, 2010, Lin signed a two-year deal with his hometown Warriors, his favorite team growing up. Lin's deal was partially guaranteed for 2010–11, and the Warriors held a team option for the second season. The deal included a first-year salary of close to $500,000 with more than half of it guaranteed. Lin said the counteroffers from the three other teams were higher, but he wanted to play for the Warriors. Lin's agent Roger Montgomery negotiated the deal. Lin also signed a three-year guaranteed contract with Nike. His jersey was already on sale before his first NBA game.

The Warriors held a press conference for Lin after his signing, with national media in attendance. "It was surprising to see that ... for an undrafted rookie," said then-Warriors coach Keith Smart. The *San Jose Mercury News* wrote that Lin "had something of a cult following" after his signing. The San Francisco Bay Area, with its large Asian-American population, celebrated his arrival. He became the first American of Chinese or Taiwanese descent to play in the NBA. Lin received the loudest ovation of the night in the Warriors' home exhibition opener at Oracle Arena when he entered the game in the fourth quarter. The crowd had started chanting for him in the third quarter and cheered whenever he touched the ball. "That really touched me. It's something I'll remember forever," Lin said. During the first month of the season, Oracle Arena fans continued to root for Lin to play in the end of games and cheered every time he touched the ball. He drew cheers from the crowd on the road as well, with some writers attributing the attention to the unique story of a successful Asian-American basketball player. Still, Lin played more relaxed on the road, where he felt less scrutiny and pressure to perform.

Lin acknowledged the expectations and warned, "I won't be an All-Star this year." He was appreciative of the support, especially from the Asian-American community, but he preferred to concentrate on his play without all the attention when he had not "proven anything to anybody." Smart saw that Lin was skilled at getting to the paint, but needed to learn to pass because, he said, Lin "couldn't shoot the ball at all". The coach also noticed that the player always arrived early for practice and left late. Lin studied and rehearsed Steve Nash and other top point guards' pick-and-roll plays. Frank Hughes of *Sports Illustrated* wrote that he talked with the occasional "seeds of self-doubt", which he said was uncommon to hear in the NBA. Hughes also found it rare when Lin compared himself to the Phoenix Suns' then-backup point guard Goran Dragić. "Neither of us is a freak athlete, but we're both effective and know how to play the game," Lin said. Lin and Stephen Curry, the 2009–10 runner-up Rookie of the Year, received more interview requests than any other Warrior.

Team officials regularly denied requests for Lin to help him keep his focus. He was approached to be the subject of documentaries. Smart planned to take pressure off Lin since Lin had a tendency to be hard on himself and get frustrated, but the coach admitted that he once succumbed to the home crowd's wishes and put Lin into a game in the wrong situation.

Lin received little playing time during the season with two dominant ball-handling guards, Curry and Monta Ellis, starring for the Warriors. He initially competed with Charlie Bell and Reggie Williams, and later Acie Law, for playing time at backup point guard. Lin started the regular season on the Warriors' inactive list, but made his NBA debut the next game during the Warriors' Asian Heritage Night. He received a standing ovation when he entered the game in the final minutes. In the next game against the Los Angeles Lakers, Lin scored his first NBA basket, had three assists, and recorded four steals. He played 11 of his 16 minutes in the third quarter and committed five fouls but played a role in a 12–1 run by the Warriors in a 107–83 loss to the defending NBA champions. Lakers' guard Derek Fisher praised Lin for his energy and aggressiveness. At Toronto on November 8, the Raptors held Asian Heritage Night to coincide with Lin's visit with the Warriors. Over 20 members of Toronto's Chinese media covered the game. In a 89–117 road loss to the Lakers, Lin scored a (then) career-high 13 points in 18 minutes after scoring only seven total points in his first six games.

Three times during the season, Lin was assigned to the Warriors' D-League affiliate, the Reno Bighorns. Each time, he was later recalled by the Warriors. He competed in the NBA D-League Showcase and was named to the All-NBA D-League Showcase First Team on January 14, 2011. Lin helped lead the Bighorns to a 2–0 record at the Showcase with averages of 21.5 points, 6.0 rebounds, 5.5 assists and 3.5 steals. Lin posted a season-high 27 points with the Bighorns on March 18. In 20 games he averaged 18 points, 5.8 rebounds and 4.4 assists with Reno. Lin initially felt he was not good enough to play in the NBA, but he later realized he was learning and getting playing time in the D-League that he would not have received with the Warriors. Lin credited Bighorns coach Eric Musselman with "helping him regain [his] swagger." Musselman recalled that Lin was a good scorer for himself but was not yet skilled at "using the whole floor". He scored many offensive fouls, but Musselman believed Lin was as good as Gilbert Arenas in the dribble drive, an ability "you can't teach". The player continued to improve his pick-and-roll, how to handle double teams and traps, and improved his jump shot and, especially, his three pointer. Musselman also noticed that Lin, who as an NBA player received first-class airplane tickets, gave them to his teammates.

The Warriors saw Lin as a potential backup for Curry. Lacob said the team received more than one trade offer for Lin while he was in the D-League, but he was happy with Lin's progress as an undrafted free agent. "He's a minimum, inexpensive asset. You need to look at him as a developing asset. Is he going to be a superstar? No." He finished his rookie NBA season averaging 2.6 points on 38.9 percent shooting in 29 games.

2011 offseason

Lin recovered from a patellar ligament injury to his knee during the 2011 NBA lockout. In September 2011, Lin played a few games for the Chinese Basketball Association (CBA) club Dongguan Leopards at the ABA Club Championship in Guangzhou, China, where he was named the MVP of the tournament. Shanghai Sharks president and former NBA star Yao Ming also tried, unsuccessfully, to sign Lin for the upcoming CBA season; Lin explained that as someone still under contract with the Golden State Warriors, he could not play in the CBA as the league would only admit NBA free agents. A few days before the lockout was lifted on November 26, Lin had been close to signing with an undisclosed club in Italy.

Lin worked to improve his jump shot during the offseason by abandoning the shooting form he had used since the eighth grade. He also increased his strength, doubling the weight he could squat (from 110 pounds (50 kg) to 231 (105)) and almost tripling the number of pull-ups that he could do (from 12 to 30). He increased his body weight from 200 pounds (91 kg) to 212 (96)—including 15 pounds (6.8 kg) of muscle—added 3.5 inches (8.9 cm) to his standing vertical jump and 6 inches (15 cm) to his running vertical jump, and improved his lateral quickness by 32 percent. Due to the lockout, he never got a chance to workout for new Warriors coach Mark Jackson. On the first day of training camp on December 9, 2011, the Warriors waived Lin. He was a favorite of Lacob, but the Warriors were freeing up salary cap space to make an offer to restricted free agent center DeAndre Jordan; Lin was due to make almost $800,000 that would have become fully guaranteed on February 10, 2012. The *San Francisco Chronicle* said Lin would have had trouble beating out rookie guard Charles Jenkins.

On December 12, 2011, Lin was claimed off waivers by the Houston Rockets. He played seven minutes in two pre-season games with the Rockets, who already had Kyle Lowry, Goran Dragić and Jonny Flynn as point guards with guaranteed contracts. On December 24, before the start of the season, the Rockets waived Lin to clear payroll to sign center Samuel Dalembert.

New York Knicks (2011–2012)

The New York Knicks claimed Lin off waivers on December 27 to be a backup behind Toney Douglas and Mike Bibby after an injury to guard Iman Shumpert; recently signed guard Baron Davis was also injured and weeks away from playing. Because of the lockout coaches had little opportunity to see Lin's play, and placed him fourth on the point guard depth chart. Lin said he was "competing for a backup spot, and people see me as the 12th to 15th guy on the roster. It's a numbers game", and continued to arrive first at practice, leave last, intensely study game film, and work with coaches to improve his footwork and judge-

Lin after his first game for the Knicks on December 28, 2011.

ment. He made his season debut on the road against the Warriors, where he was warmly cheered in his return to Oracle Arena. On January 17, 2012, Lin was assigned to the Erie BayHawks of the D-League. On January 20, he had a triple-double with 28 points, 11 rebounds, and 12 assists in the BayHawks' 122–113 victory over the Maine Red Claws. Lin was recalled by the Knicks three days later, but so feared being cut again that he asked a chaplain at a pregame prayer service to pray for him. If released again, Lin considered playing in Europe, returning to the D-League, or taking a break with a non-basketball job.

On January 28, Davis suffered a setback that postponed his Knicks debut. Then New York considered releasing Lin before his contract became guaranteed on February 10 so they could sign a new player. However, after the Knicks squandered a fourth quarter lead in a February 3 loss to the Boston Celtics, coach Mike D'Antoni decided to give Lin a chance to play, in "desperation" according to experts. "He got lucky because we were playing so bad," said D'Antoni. Lin had played only 55 minutes through the Knicks' first 23 games, but he unexpectedly led a turnaround of an 8–15 team that had lost 11 of its last 13 games.

On February 4, against the New Jersey Nets and All-Star guard Deron Williams, Lin had 25 points, five rebounds, and seven assists—all career-highs—in a 99–92 Knicks victory. Teammate Carmelo Anthony suggested to coach Mike D'Antoni at halftime that Lin should play more in the second half. After the game, D'Antoni said Lin has a point-guard mentality and "a rhyme and a reason for what he is doing out there. " In the subsequent game against the Utah Jazz, Lin made his first career start playing without stars Anthony, who left the game due to injury, and Amar'e Stoudemire, whose older brother had died. Lin had 28 points and eight assists in the Knicks' 99–88 win. Stoudemire and Anthony missed the next three and seven games, respectively. D'Antoni stated after the Jazz game that he intended to "rid[e Lin] like freakin' Secretariat." Basketball trainer David Thorpe said in hindsight that such a statement of confidence so soon by a coach was "incredibly rare", and likely gave Lin the confidence to continue to play aggressively despite making mistakes.

—Kobe Bryant, after Lin scored 38 points on February 10, 2012.

In a 107–93 win over the Washington Wizards, Lin played against John Wall and had 23 points and 10 assists, his first double-double. On February 10, Lin scored a new career-high 38 points and had seven assists, leading the Knicks in their 92–85 victory over the Los Angeles Lakers. He outscored the Lakers' Kobe Bryant, who had 34 points. On February 11, Lin scored 20 points and had 8 assists in a narrow 100–98 victory over the Minnesota Timberwolves. Lin was named the Eastern Conference Player of the Week after averaging 27.3 points, 8.3 assists and 2.0 steals in those four starts with the Knicks going undefeated.

On February 14, with less than a second remaining, Lin scored a game-winning three-pointer against the Toronto Raptors. The basket so amazed the Lakers, watching on TV, that veteran player Metta World Peace ran by reporters shouting "Linsanity! Linsanity!" and waving his hands above his head. Lin became the first NBA player to score at least 20 points and have seven assists in each of his first five starts. Lin scored 89, 109, and 136 points in his first three, four, and five career starts, respectively, all three of which are the most by any player since the merger between the American Basketball Association (ABA) and the NBA in 1976–77.

Lin shoots over former Warriors teammate David Lee.

In the following game against the Sacramento Kings, Lin recorded 13 assists and led the Knicks back to .500. New York had a 7–0 record after Lin started receiving major playing time, 6–0 with him starting. The winning streak ended in an 89–85 loss to the New Orleans Hornets; Lin scored 26 points but had nine turnovers. His 45 turnovers in his first seven career starts were the most since individual turnovers began being tracked in 1977–78. On February 19 in a 104–97 win against the Mavericks, Lin scored 28 points and tallied career highs with 14 assists and five steals. USA Today wrote, "No matter what Dallas threw at Lin – double-teams, traps, blitzes, tall defenders ... smaller defenders ... stocky, thin – Lin found a way ... to a victory against the defending NBA champions." He did not do as well on February 23 against LeBron James' Miami Heat, going one for eight from the field and committing eight turnovers. The eventual NBA champions focused their entire defense on Lin, an experience he described as "flattering—and terrifying ... I felt like they were all like hawks circling me and staring."

In his 12 starts before the All-Star break, Lin averaged 22.5 points and 8.7 assists, and New York had a 9–3 record. He played in the Rising Stars Challenge during NBA All-Star Weekend. He was omitted from the original Rising Stars roster, but was added after his sudden rise to stardom. Some media outlets—including *USA Today*, *Los Angeles Times*, and *CBSSports.com*—stated that he deserved to play in the All-Star Game.

The Knicks in March replaced D'Antoni with Mike Woodson, who ran fewer pick-and rolls and more isolation plays. Lin had excelled running pick-and-rolls under D'Antoni. After the March 24 game against the Detroit Pistons he complained about a sore knee, and an MRI later revealed a small meniscus tear in the left knee. Lin opted to have knee surgery and missed the remainder of the regular season. He averaged 18.5 points and 7.6 assists during his 26 games as an everyday player. In the first 10 games, Lin averaged 24.6 points and 9.2 assists, shooting 49.7 percent from the field but with 5.6 turnovers. In the next seven games, he averaged 16 points and 7.7 assists with 3.9 turnovers. In the last nine games, Lin averaged 13.6 points and 5.9 assists and shot only 39.1 percent while dealing with his then-undisclosed knee injury.

Lin became a restricted free agent at the end of the season. The *New York Times* called Lin "[the Knicks'] most popular player in a decade", but his success over only 26 games left teams uncertain about his overall standing among the league's point guards. Some still believed Lin was a bench player.

Houston Rockets (2012–present)

The Knicks encouraged Lin to seek other offers, but he and the press expected that the team would resign him given its need for a young guard, his good play, and worldwide popularity; ESPN reported that the Knicks would match any other offer "up to $1 billion". The Rockets offered a $28.8 million contract over four years with the fourth year of that deal being at the team's option, which put the true commitment at $19.5 million. Woodson said the Knicks would match Houston's offer and that Lin would be his starting point guard. The Rockets offered a revised three-year, $25 million deal which the Knicks did not match; Lin deduced the team's decision when he learned that the Knicks signed Raymond Felton instead. The first two years of his contract pay $5 million and $5.225 million, respectively, followed by $14.8 million in the third year. The higher salary in the final year, known as a "poison pill", was intended to discourage New York from matching the offer. Including luxury tax, the Knicks' cost for Lin in 2014–15 was estimated at $43 million. The Knicks' failure to match the offer nonetheless greatly surprised observers, given the team's history of high payrolls; Lin would only have been the fourth highest-paid Knick.

Career statistics

College

Year	Team	GP	GS	MPG	FG%
2006–07	Harvard	28	0	18.1	.415
2007–08	Harvard	**30**	**30**	31.3	.448
2008–09	Harvard	28	28	**34.8**	.502
2009–10	Harvard	29	29	32.2	**.519**
Career		115	87	29.2	.481

NBA
Regular season

Year	Team	GP	GS	MPG	FG%
2010–11	Golden State	29	0	9.8	.389
2011–12	New York	**35**	25	26.9	**.446**
Career		64	25	19.7	.437

International career

In addition to being a U.S. citizen, Lin is also by descent through his parents a national of the Republic of China (Taiwan); Lin could apply for a Republic

Lin at a press conference in Taiwan

of China passport although there is no record of his having done so. Lin has been invited to play for the Chinese Taipei men's national basketball team in FIBA competitions. On July 28, 2010 while in Taipei to play in Yao Ming's charity game, Lin said he had not made a decision yet on whether he would represent Chinese Taipei (the name used by Taiwan in international sporting competitions). In June 2011, the Chinese Taipei Basketball Association (CTBA) included Lin in its preliminary squad of 24 players for the 2011 FIBA Asia Championship. The next month, however, the CTBA announced that Lin would not be included on their roster due to a knee injury.

Taiwanese media reported that Lin declined an offer from the People's Republic of China to play in the same tournament; however, the Chinese Basketball Management Center denied having ever approached him.

Lin was named to the USA Basketball Men's Select Team to scrimmage against the 2012 USA Olympic team candidates, but he did not participate due to his restricted free agent status with the Knicks.

Racial issues

Sean Gregory of *Time* wrote of Lin's zero Division I scholarship offers: "[Lin] was scrawny, but don't doubt that a little racial profiling, intentional or otherwise, contributed to his underrecruitment." Diepenbrock stated, "If [Lin] was African American or Caucasian, it might have been a different deal"; he did not think Lin's race affected his recruiting until later seeing 10 Division I coaches express interest in a black student who Diepenbrock assessed as "a nice junior college player." Lin said: "I'm not saying top-5 state automatically gets you offers, but I do think (my ethnicity) did affect the way coaches recruited me. I think if I were a different race, I would've been treated differently." Walters added, "People who don't think stereotypes exist are crazy. If [Lin's] white, he's either a good shooter or heady. If he's Asian, he's good at math. We're not taking him."

Diepenbrock said that people without meaning any harm assume since Lin is Asian that he is not a basketball player. The first time Lin went to a Pro-Am game in Kezar Pavilion in San Francisco someone there informed him: "Sorry, sir, there's no volleyball here tonight. It's basketball." During Lin's college career, fewer than 0.5% of men's Division 1 basketball players were Asian-American. Lin has regularly heard bigoted jeers at games such as "Wonton soup", "Sweet and sour pork", "Open your eyes!", "Go back to China", "Orchestra is on the other side of campus", or pseudo-Chinese gibberish. Lin says this occurred at most if not all Ivy League gyms. He does not react to it. "I expect it, I'm used to it, it is what it is," says Lin. The heckling came mostly from opposing fans and not as much from players. According to Harvard teammate Oliver McNally, a fellow Ivy League player once called Lin the ethnic slur *chink*. In January 2010, Harvard played against Santa Clara University at the Leavey Center, just 15 miles from his hometown of Palo Alto, California. Playing to a capacity crowd that included droves of Asian Americans wanting to see his homecoming, his teammates told him, "It was like Hong Kong."

Lin considers himself a basketball player more than just an Asian American. He understands that there have not been many Asians in the NBA. "Maybe I can help break the stereotype," said Lin. "I feel like Asians in general don't get the respect that we may deserve whether it comes to sports, basketball, or whatever it might be." Prior to the 2010–11 NBA season, Americans of Asian descent who played in the NBA included Wataru Misaka, Raymond Townsend, Corey Gaines, Rex Walters, and Robert Swift. "[Lin's] carrying the hopes of an entire continent. I only had to carry the hopes of Little Rock, Arkansas. He's accomplished a lot more than I have already," said Derek Fisher, who had won five NBA championships with the Lakers, after his first game against Lin. Lin is setting an example for prospective Asian athletes in America who rarely see Asian-Americans playing on their favorite teams. "I don't look Japanese," Walters said, referring to his mother's ethnicity. "When they see [Lin], it's an Asian-American".

Some fans and commentators wrote off his Warriors signing as a publicity stunt. Larry Riley, the team's general manager, denied catering to the Bay Area's large Asian population. He understood that some people would see it that way. "We evaluated him throughout summer league," Riley said. "All that had to happen was for him to confirm what we already believed." While the team created a campaign around him, Riley said it would not have been advisable if Lin was not a basketball player first.
—Jeremy Lin, during 2012 All-Star Weekend interview
On February 10, 2012, in the middle of Lin's career game against the Lakers, Fox Sports columnist Jason Whitlock posted on Twitter, "Some lucky lady in NYC is gonna feel a couple inches of pain tonight", a reference to Lin's sexual prowess. *Hyphen* wrote that Whitlock "reinforced the insipid and insidious 'small Asian penis' stereotype." The Asian American Journalists Association demanded an apology. "I debased a feel-good sports moment. For that, I'm truly sorry," apologized Whitlock. Boxer Floyd Mayweather, Jr. wrote on his Twitter page, "Jeremy Lin is a good player but all the hype is because he's Asian. Black players do what he does every night and don't get the same praise." *NBCNewYork.com* in response to Mayweather noted that "no one of any skin color in the history of basketball has done in their first four starts what Lin pulled off for the Knicks last week." On February 15, the MSG Network during game coverage showed a fan's sign of Lin's face above a fortune cookie with the words "The Knicks Good Fortune", which some viewed as an ethnic stereotype. *Sporting News* wrote that the sign was "questionable", while CBS News called it "distasteful". Some Knicks teammates have been criticized for bowing to Lin during games. On February 17, ESPN used a racial slur on its mobile website in the headline "Chink in the Armor" after Lin had nine turnovers in New York's loss to the Hornets. It was removed 35 minutes later, and ESPN apologized. The network fired the employee who posted the headline, and suspended ESPNews anchor Max Bretos for using the same reference earlier in the week. Bretos also apologized. Knicks radio announcer Spero Dedes also used the phrase on 1050 ESPN New York, but he was an employee of Madison Square Garden (MSG) and not ESPN. He apologized and was disciplined by MSG. *Saturday Night Live* in a cold open satirized the puns in reference to Lin's ethnicity; three commentators were featured happily making jokes about Lin's race, while a fourth drew contempt for making similar comments about black players. ESPN received emails suggesting that Lin was subjected to racial slurs in a manner that African-Americans are not. Ben & Jerry's created a frozen yogurt in honor of Lin named "Taste the Lin-Sanity". The company replaced the fortune cookies with waffle cookies and apologized to anyone offended by their Lin-Sanity flavor. J. A. Adande of ESPN.com wrote that the heightened ethnic sensitivity toward Asian Americans was "another way [Lin's] impact resonates far beyond Madison Square Garden." The AAJA released a set of guidelines to the media in response to what it termed as "factual inaccuracies about Lin's background as well as an alarming number of references that rely on stereotypes about Asians or Asian Americans."

Public image

Lin has a YouTube account, and has

made videos with YouTube personalities Nigahiga and KevJumba. Lin and former Knicks teammate Landry Fields eventually appeared on a video on Lin's YouTube Channel revealing their "secret handshake". In a video interview conducted by Elie Seckbach, he asked Lin how it felt to be representing so many people. Lin responded by stating, "It's humbling, a privilege, and a honor. I'm really proud of being Chinese, I'm really proud of my parents being from Taiwan. I just thank God for the opportunity." In July 2011, the overseas Chinese *Vivid Magazine* named Lin one of its top eight influential Chinese-Americans. In April 2012, Lin was named to *Time Magazine'*s 2012 list of the "Top 100 Most Influential People in the World." On June 18, 2012, NBA TV announced that Lin was the first-ever winner of the "Social Breakout Player of the Year" Award. He was also the winner of "The EPIC Award".

"Linsanity"

    External images

 Lin on February 20, 2012 cover of *Sports Illustrated*

 Lin on February 27, 2012 cover of *Sports Illustrated*

 Lin on February 27, 2012 cover of *Time*

After he became a starter for the Knicks, the Associated Press called Lin "the most surprising story in the NBA". *Bloomberg News* wrote that Lin "has already become the most famous [Asian American NBA player]". Knicks fans developed nicknames for him along with a new lexicon inspired by his name, *Lin*. Most popular was the word *Linsanity*, the excitement over the unheralded Lin. *Time.com* ran an article titled, "It's Official: Linsanity Is for Real". Hall of Fame player Magic Johnson said, "The excitement [Lin] has caused in [Madison Square] Garden, man, I hadn't seen that in a long time." He appeared on the cover of *Sports Illustrated* with the headline "Against All Odds", which the *Times* called "the greatest tribute". He also made the cover of *Time* in Asia; *Forbes* wrote, "Congratulations Jeremy. You have now made the cover of *Time* the same number of times as Michael Jordan. Linsanity reigns on." Lin's story was also on the front-page of many Taipei newspapers. "I haven't done a computation, but it's fair to say that no player has created the interest and the frenzy in this short period of time, in any sport, that I'm aware of like Jeremy Lin has," said NBA commissioner David Stern.

Lin's jersey on display

The Knicks' success due to Lin's play reportedly contributed to the end of a dispute which had for 48 days prevented Time Warner Cable customers from watching Knicks games and other MSG Network programs. The team quickly began selling replicas of Lin's No. 17 jerseys and t-shirts, and the sales and traffic for its online store increased more than 3,000%; Lin's merchandise dominated the displays at Knicks stores, with those for the team's high-priced stars—Anthony, Stoudemire, and Tyson Chandler—were moved to the sale racks. He had the best selling jersey in the NBA in February and March. For the one-year period ending April 2012, Lin had the second highest selling jersey in the league behind Derrick Rose. Both Nike and Adidas introduced Lin-related athletic apparel, and expected that his fame would help sales in China. His popularity was attributed with growing the NBA's popularity there since Yao Ming's retirement in the offseason; the audience for NBA games on television and online in China rose 39 percent over the previous season.

Within three weeks of his first game as a starter, at least seven e-books were being published on Lin, and the Global Language Monitor declared that *Linsanity* had met its criteria to be considered an English-language word. He appeared on a second consecutive *Sports Illustrated* cover, the first New York-based team athlete and the third NBA player in the magazine's history, after Jordan and Dirk Nowitzki. New York City restaurants introduced new food and bar items in honor or Lin. The city has about 450,000 residents of Chinese or Taiwanese descent—larger than the entire populations of NBA cities like Miami, Atlanta or Cleveland—and viewing parties to watch Lin play flourished in Manhattan's Chinatown. An airline advertised "Linsanely low prices", bids for his rookie card exceeded $21,000 on eBay, and the press circulated rumors—denied by Lin—that he was dating Kim Kardashian. *Foreign Policy* speculated on his potential impact on Sino-American relations, and Jack and Suzy Welch wrote that Lin's rise was a lesson to business leaders to not let bureaucracy stifle unproven talent. Despite his sudden fame Sacramento Kings coach Keith Smart stated, "I knew [Lin] before he was Linmania. He's still the same humble guy. The guy has not changed a bit, which is real special for a young man."

Endorsements

Volvo
Nike
Steiner Sports

Personal life

Lin is an evangelical Christian who was a leader in Harvard's Asian American Christian Fellowship during his time there. He credited his NBA success to playing without pressure. "I've surrendered that to God. I'm not in a battle with what everybody else thinks anymore," said Lin. He hopes to become a pastor who can head up non-profit organizations, either home or abroad, and has talked of working in inner-city communities to help with underprivileged children. Lin's younger brother, Joseph, plays basketball for Hamilton College, and his older brother, Josh, is a dental student at New York University.

When Lin was asked if he was fluent

in Chinese, he stated that he could understand it, but could use some help speaking it. In an interview conducted with NBADraft.net, Lin stated that he could only speak Mandarin, not Cantonese, and could read and write a little. He had also taken classes while attending Harvard to try to improve. Lin in early 2012 slept on his brother's couch in a one-bedroom apartment on the Lower East Side of Manhattan, New York City. The night before his breakout game, he slept on the couch of teammate Landry Fields. He relocated to a luxury condo in White Plains, New York, after his Knicks contract became guaranteed.

Source http://en.wikipedia.org/wiki/Jeremy_Lin

Keith Wright (basketball)

Keith Wright

College	Harvard
Conference	Ivy League
Sport	Basketball
Position	Forward
Jersey #	44
Height	6 ft 8 in (2.03 m)
Weight	240 lb (109 kg)
Nationality	American
High school	Norfolk Collegiate School Princess Anne High School

Awards

Ivy League Player of the Year (2011)

Keith Wright is an American basketball player, most recently playing for the NCAA Division I Harvard Crimson.

High School

Wright attended Princess Anne High School and Norfolk Collegiate School, where he graduated from. As a senior, he averaged 20.5 points, 13.0 rebounds and 3.5 blocks per game. In high school, Wright was a two-time All-State selection.

College career

Freshman Season

In Wright's freshman season, he appeared in 24 games, including 17 starts. He averaged 8.0 points per game and 5.5 rebounds per game. He was named Ivy League Rookie of the Week twice.

Sophomore season

Wright appeared in 24 games, starting in 18. During his sophomore season, Wright averaged 8.9 points per game and 4.6 rebounds per game. During this season, Harvad made the CollegeInsider.com Postseason Tournament. Harvard lost in the first round of the tournament to Appalachian State.

Junior season

In his junior season at Harvard, Wright played well enough to be named the 2011 Ivy League Men's Basketball Player of the Year, after leading the Crimson in scoring at 14.8 points per game and rebounding at 8.3 rebounds per game. Wright was also a unanimous selection to the Men's Basketball All-Ivy First Team. In Wright's junior season, Harvard made the National Invitation Tournament for the first time in school history, but lost in the first round to Oklahoma State. In the game, Wright recorded ten points and four rebounds.

Senior season

Prior to his senior season, Wright was named to the Wooden Award preseason top 50 watch list. He was also named the preseason Ivy League Player of the Year by Rivals.com, Athlon Sports, and Sporting News. Wright was a co-captain with Oliver McNally. In Wright's senior season, he averaged 10.6 points per game and 8.1 rebounds per game. He also became the Crimson's all-time leading shot blocker. This was good enough for Wright to be named to the Men's Basketball All-Ivy League second team. In the 2011-12 season, Harvard made the NCAA Men's Basketball Tournament for the first time since 1946. Harvard lost to the Vanderbilt Commodores in the round of 64, with Wright recording eight points and nine rebounds. After the season ended, Wright was chosen to play in the Reese's All-Star Game. Wright recorded seven points and six rebounds in the game. Wright also participated in the Portsmouth Invitational Tournament.

Professional career

After going undrafted in the 2012 NBA Draft, Wright agreed to play with the Dallas Mavericks in the NBA Summer League.

Source http://en.wikipedia.org/wiki/Keith_Wright_(basketball)

Lou Silver

Medal record

Competitor for		Israel
Men's Basketball		
European Championships		
Silver	1979 Italy	Team Competition

Louis Grant Silver (born circa 1953) is a businessperson and attorney having retired from a career as a professional American-Israeli basketball player. Lou received his A.B. from Harvard College in 1975, LL.B. from Tel Aviv University School of Law and LL.M. from New York University School of Law.

During his basketball career, Lou played at power forward positions (height 2.03m) and was considered an "all-around" player. Lou played his college ball for Harvard College and was selected by the Kentucky Colonels in the 8th round (73rd overall) of the 1975 American Basketball Association Draft. Lou served as Co-Captain during his final year at Harvard College and received a number of accolades while attending, and playing for, Harvard College including being selected for All Ivy League and Division honors.

Lou played for Maccabi Tel Aviv (1975–1985) and served as a Captain of the team from 1981-1985. While playing for Maccabi Tel Aviv, the team won 10 Israeli League Championships (1976, 1977, 1978, 1979, 1980, 1981, 1982, 1983, 1984, 1985) and 8 Israeli State Cups (1977, 1978, 1979, 1980, 1981, 1982, 1983, 1985). Lou was a key member of the Maccabi teams which reached 4 European Champions Cup finals winning 2 European Champions Cup titles (1977 and 1981) and the Intercontinental Cup in 1981.

Lou also played for, and led, the Israeli National Team to a second place finish in the European Championships for National Teams winning the Silver Medal while losing to the Soviet Union National Team in the finals at Eurobasket 1979 in Italy. Lou was selected to the European Selection All Star Team in the early 1980s playing with the Selection Team in Ankara and Barcelona. In 1987, FIBA honoured Lou with a retirement game featuring Maccabi Tel Aviv against the then European Selection Team.

Following his retirement from basketball, Lou has practiced Corporate Law at Stroock & Stroock & Lavan in New York City and served as General Counsel to a publicly listed software company based in Paris, France. His professional career includes profiles as an investment banker, private banker and hedge fund manager. Lou continues to serve as a member of the Board of Directors of a number of publicly listed and privately held companies actively involved in Corporate Governance, Audit and Compensation Committees.

Source http://en.wikipedia.org/wiki/Lou_Silver

Michael Crichton

Michael Crichton

Michael Crichton at Harvard University (April 18, 2002)

Born	John Michael Crichton October 23, 1942 Chicago, Illinois, U.S.
Died	November 4, 2008 (aged Los Angeles, California,
Pen name	John Lange Jeffery Hudson Michael Douglas
Occupation	Author, film producer, fil rector, screenwriter, telev producer
Language	English
Nationality	American
Education	Harvard College Harvard Medical School
Period	1966–2008
Genres	Action, adventure, scienc tion, techno-thriller
Notable award(s)	1969 Edgar Award
Signature	

www.crichton-official.com

John Michael Crichton (/ˈkraɪtən/; rhymes with *frighten*; October 23, 1942 – November 4, 2008) was an American best-selling author, producer, director, and screenwriter, best known for his work in the science fiction, medical fiction, and thriller genres. His books have sold over 200 million copies worldwide, and many have been adapted into films. In 1994, Crichton became the only creative artist ever to have works simultaneously charting at No. 1 in television, film, and book sales (with *ER*, *Jurassic Park*, and *Disclosure*, respectively).

His literary works are usually based on the action genre and heavily feature technology. His novels epitomize the techno-thriller genre of literature, often exploring technology and failures of human interaction with it, especially resulting in catastrophes with biotechnology. Many of his future history novels have medical or scientific underpinnings, reflecting his medical training and science background. He was the author of, among others, *Jurassic Park*, *The Andromeda Strain*, *Congo*, *Travels*, *Sphere*, *Rising Sun*, *Disclosure*, *The Lost World*, *Airframe*, *Timeline*, *Prey*, *State of Fear*, *Next* (the final book published before his death), *Pirate Latitudes* (published November 24, 2009), and a final unfinished techno-thriller, *Micro*, which was published in November 2011.

Early life and education

John Michael Crichton was born in Chicago Illinois, to John Henderson Crichton, a journalist, and Zula Miller Crichton, on October 23, 1942. He was raised on Long Island, in Roslyn, New York, and had three siblings: two sisters, Kimberly and Catherine, and a younger brother, Douglas. Crichton showed a keen interest in writing from a young age and at the age of 14 had a column related to travel published in *The New York Times*. Crichton had always planned on becoming a writer and began his studies at Harvard College in 1960. During his undergraduate study in literature, he conducted an experiment to expose a professor whom he believed to be giving him abnormally low marks and criticizing his literary style. Informing another professor of his suspicions, Crichton plagiarized a work by George Orwell and submitted it as his own. The paper was returned by his unwitting professor with a mark of "B−". His issues with the English department led Crichton to switch his concentration to biological anthropology as an undergraduate, obtaining his A.B. *summa cum laude* in 1964. He was also initiated into the Phi Beta Kappa Society. He went on to become the Henry Russell Shaw Traveling Fellow from 1964 to 1965 and Visiting Lecturer in Anthropology at the University of Cambridge in the United Kingdom in 1965.

Crichton later enrolled at Harvard Medical School, when he began publishing work. By this time he had become exceptionally tall. By his own account, he was approximately 6 feet 9 inches (2.06 m) tall in 1997. In reference to his height, while in medical school, he began writing novels under the pen names "John Lange" and "Jeffrey Hudson" ("Lange" is a surname in Germany, meaning "long", and Sir Jeffrey Hudson was a famous 17th-century dwarf in the court of Queen Consort Henrietta Maria of England). In *Travels*, he recalls overhearing doctors who were unaware that he was the author, discussing the flaws in his book *The Andromeda Strain*. *A Case of Need*, written under the Hudson pseudonym, won him his first Edgar Award for Best Novel in 1969. He also co-authored *Dealing* with his younger brother Douglas under the shared pen name "Michael Douglas". The back cover of that book carried a picture, taken by their mother, of Michael and Douglas when very young.

During his clinical rotations at the Boston City Hospital, Crichton grew disenchanted with the culture there, which appeared to emphasize the interests and reputations of doctors over the interests of patients. Crichton graduated from Harvard, obtaining an M.D. in 1969, and undertook a post-doctoral fellowship study at the Salk Institute for Biological Studies in La Jolla, California, from 1969 to 1970. He never obtained a license to practice medicine, devoting himself to his writing career instead.

Reflecting on his career in medicine years later, Crichton concluded that patients too often shunned responsibility for their own health, relying on doctors as miracle workers rather than advisors. He experimented with astral projection, aura viewing, and clairvoyance, coming to believe that these included real phenomena that scientists had too eagerly dismissed as paranormal.

In 1988, Crichton was a visiting writer at the Massachusetts Institute of Technology.

Writing career

Fiction

Odds On was Michael Crichton's first published novel. It was published in 1966, under the pseudonym of John Lange. It is a 215-page paperback novel which describes an attempted robbery in an isolated hotel on Costa Brava. The robbery is planned scientifically with the help of a Critical Path Analysis computer program, but unforeseen events get in the way.

The following year, he published *Scratch One*. The novel relates the story of Roger Carr, a handsome, charming and privileged man who practices law, more as a means to support his playboy lifestyle than a career. Carr is sent to Nice, France, where he has notable political connections, but is mistaken for an assassin and finds his life in jeopardy, implicated in the world of terrorism.

In 1968, he published two novels, *Easy Go* and *A Case of Need*, the second of which was re-published in 1993, under his real name. *Easy Go* relates the story of Harold Barnaby, a brilliant Egyptologist, who discovers a concealed message while translating hieroglyphics, informing him of an unnamed Pharaoh whose tomb is yet to be discovered. *A Case of Need*, on the other hand, was a medical thriller in which a Boston pathologist, Dr. John Berry, investigates an apparent illegal abortion conducted by an obstetrician friend, which caused the early demise of a young woman. The novel would prove a turning point in Crichton's future novels, in which technology is important in the subject matter, although this novel was as much about medical practice. The novel earned him an Edgar Award in 1969.

In 1969, Crichton published three novels. The first, *Zero Cool*, dealt with an American radiologist on vacation in Spain who is caught in a murderous crossfire between rival gangs seeking a precious artifact. The second, *The Andromeda Strain*, would prove to be the most important novel of his career and establish him as a best-selling author. The novel documented the efforts of a team of scientists investigating a deadly extraterrestrial microorganism that fatally clots human blood, infecting the sufferer and causing death within two minutes. The microbe, code named "Andromeda", mutates with each growth cycle, changing its biological properties. The novel became an instant success, and it was only two years before the novel was sought after by film producers and turned into the 1971 film under the direction of Robert Wise and featuring Arthur Hill, James Olson, Kate Reid as Leavitt, and David Wayne. In September 2004, the Sci Fi Channel would announce a production of a miniseries, executive-produced by Ridley Scott, Tony Scott and Frank Darabont, premiering on May 26, 2008. Crichton's third novel of 1969, *The Venom Business* relates the story of a smuggler who uses his exceptional skill as a snake handler to his advantage by importing snakes to be used by drug companies and universities for medical research. The snakes are simply a ruse to hide the presence of rare Mexican artifacts. In 1969, Crichton also wrote a review for *The New Republic* (as J. Michael Crichton), critiquing *Slaughterhouse Five* by Kurt Vonnegut.

In 1970, Crichton again published three novels: *Drug of Choice*, *Dealing: Or the Berkeley-to-Boston Forty-Brick Lost-Bag Blues* and *Grave Descend*. *Grave Descend* earned him an Edgar Award nomination the following year.

In 1972, Crichton published two novels. The first, *Binary*, relates the story of a villainous middle-class businessman, who attempts to assassinate the President of the United States by stealing an army shipment of the two precursor chemicals that form a deadly nerve agent. The second, *The Terminal Man*, is about a psychomotor epileptic sufferer, Harry Benson, who in regularly suffering seizures followed by blackouts, conducts himself inappropriately during seizures, waking up hours later with no knowledge of what he has done. Believed to be psychotic, he is investigated; electrodes are implanted in his brain, continuing the preoccupation in Crichton's novels with machine-human interaction and technology. The novel was adapted into a film directed by Mike Hodges and starring George Segal, Joan Hackett, Richard A. Dysart and Donald Moffat, released in June 1974. However, neither the novel nor the film was well received by critics.

In 1975, Crichton ventured into the nineteenth century with his historical novel *The Great Train Robbery*, which would become a bestseller. The novel is a recreation of the Great Gold Robbery of 1855, a massive gold heist, which takes place on a train traveling through Victorian era England. A considerable proportion of the book was set in London. The novel was later made into a 1979 film directed by Crichton himself, starring Sean Connery and Donald Sutherland. The film would go on to be nominated for Best Cinematography Award by the British Society of Cinematographers, also garnering an Edgar Allan Poe Award for Best Motion Picture by the Mystery Writers Association of America.

In 1976, Crichton published *Eaters of the Dead*, a novel about a tenth-century Muslim who travels with a group of Vikings to their settlement. *Eaters of the Dead* is narrated as a scientific commentary on an old manuscript and was inspired by two sources. The first three chapters retell Ahmad ibn Fadlan's personal account of his journey north and his experiences in encountering the Rus', the early Russian peoples, whilst the remainder is based upon the story of Beowulf, culminating in battles with the 'mist-monsters', or 'wendol', a relict group of Neanderthals. The novel was adapted into film as *The 13th Warrior*, initially directed by John McTiernan, who was later fired with Crichton himself taking over direction.

In 1980, Crichton published the novel *Congo*, which centers on an expedition searching for diamonds in the tropical rain forest of Congo. They discover the legendary lost city of Zinj and an unusual race of barbarous gorillas. The novel was loosely adapted into a 1995 film, starring Laura Linney, Tim Curry, and Ernie Hudson.

Seven years later, Crichton published *Sphere*, a novel which relates the story of psychologist Norman Johnson, who is required by the U.S. Navy to join a team of scientists assembled by the U. S. Government to examine an enormous alien spacecraft discovered on the bed of the Pacific Ocean, and believed to have been there for over 300 years. The novel begins as a science fiction story, but rapidly changes into a psychological thriller, ultimately exploring the nature of the human imagination. The novel was adapted into the film *Sphere* in 1998, directed by Barry Levinson, with a cast including Dustin Hoffman as Norman Johnson, (renamed Norman Goodman), Samuel L. Jackson, Liev Schreiber and Sharon Stone.

In 1990, Crichton published the novel *Jurassic Park*. Crichton utilized the presentation of "fiction as fact", used in his previous novels, *Eaters of the Dead* and *The Andromeda Strain*. In addition, chaos theory and its philosophical implications are used to explain the collapse of an amusement park in a "biological preserve" on Isla Nublar, an island west of Costa Rica. Paleontologist Alan Grant and his paleobotanist graduate student, Ellie Sattler, are brought in by billionaire John Hammond to investigate. The park is revealed to contain genetically recreated dinosaur species, including *Dilophosaurus*, *Velociraptor*, *Triceratops*, *Stegosaurus*, and *Tyrannosaurus rex*, among others. They have been recreated using damaged dinosaur DNA, found in mosquitoes that sucked Saurian blood and were then trapped and preserved in amber.

Crichton had originally conceived a

Crichton's novel *Jurassic Park* and its sequels made into films would become a part of popular culture, with related parks established in places as far afield as Kletno, Poland.

screenplay about a graduate student who recreates a dinosaur, but decided to explore his fascination with dinosaurs and cloning until he began writing the novel. Spielberg learned of the novel in October 1989, while he and Crichton were discussing a screenplay that would become the television series *ER*. Before the book was published, Crichton demanded a non-negotiable fee of $1.5 million as well as a substantial percentage of the gross. Warner Bros. and Tim Burton, Sony Pictures Entertainment and Richard Donner, and 20th Century Fox and Joe Dante bid for the rights, but Universal eventually acquired them in May 1990, for Spielberg. Universal paid Crichton a further $500,000 to adapt his own novel, which he had completed by the time Spielberg was filming *Hook*. Crichton noted that because the book was "fairly long", his script only had about 10–20 percent of the novel's content. The film, directed by Spielberg, was eventually released in 1993, starring Sam Neill as Dr. Alan Grant, Laura Dern as Dr. Ellie Sattler, Jeff Goldblum as Dr. Ian Malcolm (the chaos theorist), and Richard Attenborough, as John Hammond, the billionaire CEO, of InGen. The film would go on to become extremely successful.

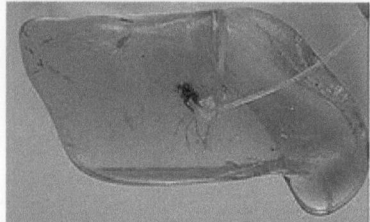

A mosquito preserved in amber. A specimen of this sort was the source of dinosaur DNA in *Jurassic Park*.

In 1992, Crichton published the novel *Rising Sun*, an international best-selling crime thriller about a murder in the Los Angeles headquarters of Nakamoto, a fictional Japanese corporation. The book was instantly adapted into a film, released the same year of the movie adaption of *Jurassic Park* in 1993, and starring Sean Connery, Wesley Snipes, Tia Carrere and Harvey Keitel.

His next novel, *Disclosure*, published in 1994, addresses the theme of sexual harassment previously explored in his 1972 *Binary*. Unlike that novel however, Crichton centers on sexual politics in the workplace, emphasizing an array of paradoxes in traditional gender functions, by featuring a male protagonist who is being sexually harassed by a female executive. As a result, the book has been harshly criticized by feminist commentators and accused of anti-feminism. Crichton, anticipating this response, offered a rebuttal at the close of the novel which states that a "role-reversal" story uncovers aspects of the subject that would not be as easily seen with a female protagonist. The novel was made into a film the same year under the helm of Barry Levinson, and starring Michael Douglas, Demi Moore and Donald Sutherland.

Crichton then published *The Lost World* in 1995, as the sequel to *Jurassic Park*. It was made into a film sequel two years later in 1997, again directed by Spielberg and starring Jeff Goldblum, Julianne Moore, Vince Vaughn and Pete Postlethwaite.

Then, in 1996, Crichton published *Airframe*, an aero-techno-thriller which relates the story of a quality assurance vice-president at the fictional aerospace manufacturer Norton Aircraft, as she investigates an in-flight accident aboard a Norton-manufactured airliner that leaves three passengers dead and fifty-six injured. Again, Crichton uses the false document literary device, presenting numerous technical documents to create a sense of authenticity. In the novel, Crichton draws from real life accidents to increase its sensation of realism, including American Airlines Flight 191 and Aeroflot Flight 593; the latter flew from Moscow's Sheremetyevo International Airport and crashed on its way to Hong Kong's Kai Tak Airport in 1994. Crichton challenges the public perception of air safety and the consequences of exaggerated media reports to sell the story. The book also continues Crichton's overall theme of the failure of humans in human-machine interaction, given that the plane itself worked perfectly and the accident would not have occurred had the pilot reacted properly.

In 1999, Crichton published *Timeline*, a science fiction novel which tells the story of a team of historians and archaeologists studying a site in the Dordogne region of France, where the medieval towns of Castelgard and La Roque stood. They time travel back to 1357 to uncover some startling truths. The novel, which continues Crichton's long history of combining technical details and action in his books, addresses quantum physics and time travel directly and received a warm welcome from medieval scholars, who praised his depiction of the challenges in studying the Middle Ages.

The novel quickly spawned Timeline Computer Entertainment, a computer game developer that created the *Timeline* PC game published by Eidos Interactive in 2000. A *film* based on the book was released in 2003, by Paramount Pictures, with a screen adaptation by Jeff Maguire and George Nolfi, under the direction of Richard Donner. The film stars Paul Walker, Gerard Butler and Frances O'Connor.

In 2002, Crichton published *Prey*, a cautionary tale about developments in science and technology; specifically nanotechnology. The novel explores relatively recent phenomena engendered by the work of the scientific community, such as artificial life, emergence (and by extension, complexity), genetic algorithms, and agent-based computing. Reiterating components in many of his other novels, Crichton once again devises fictional companies, this time Xymos, a nanorobotics company which is claimed to be on the verge of perfecting a revolutionary new medical imaging technology based on nanotechnology and a rival company, Media-Tronics.

In 2004, Crichton published *State of Fear*, a novel concerning eco-terrorists who attempt mass murder to support their views. Global warming serves as a central theme to the novel, although review in Nature found it *likely to mislead the unwary*. The novel had an initial print run of 1.5 million copies and reached the No. 1 bestseller position at Amazon.com and No. 2 on *The New York Times* Best Seller list for one week in January 2005.

The last novel published while he was still living was *Next*, printed in 2006. The novel follows many characters, including transgenic animals, in the quest to survive in a world dominated by genetic research, corporate greed, and legal interventions, wherein government and private investors spend billions of dollars every year on genetic research.

His last novel, *Pirate Latitudes*, was originally scheduled for a release date of December 2, 2008. However, it was postponed until November 24, 2009. Additionally, an unfinished novel, titled *Micro*, was published on November 22, 2011. The novel has been co-written by Richard Preston.

Non-fiction

Aside from fiction, Crichton wrote several other books based on medical or scientific themes, often based upon his own observations in his field of expertise. In 1970, he published *Five Patients*, a book which recounts his experiences of hospital practices in the late 1960s at Massachusetts General Hospi-

Crichton's first published book of non-fiction, *Five Patients*, recounts his experiences of practices in the late 1960s at Massachusetts General Hospital and the issues of costs and politics within the American Healthcare Service.

tal in Boston, Massachusetts. The book follows each of five patients through their hospital experience and the context of their treatment, revealing inadequacies in the hospital institution at the time. The book relates the experiences of Ralph Orlando, a construction worker seriously injured in a scaffold collapse; John O'Connor, a middle aged dispatcher suffering from fever that has reduced him to a delirious wreck; Peter Luchesi, a young man who severs his hand in an accident; Sylvia Thompson, an airline passenger who suffers chest pains; and Edith Murphy, a mother of three who is diagnosed with a life threatening disease. In *Five Patients*, Crichton examines a brief history of medicine up to 1969, to help place hospital culture and practice into context, and addresses the costs and politics of the national healthcare service.

As a personal friend of the artist Jasper Johns, Crichton compiled many of his works in a coffee table book, published as *Jasper Johns*. It was originally published in 1970, by Harry N. Abrams, Inc. in association with the Whitney Museum of American Art, and again in January 1977, with a second revised edition published in 1994.

In 1983, Crichton authored *Electronic Life*, a book that introduces BASIC programming to its readers. The book, written like a glossary, with entries such as "Afraid of Computers (everybody is)," "Buying a Computer," and "Computer Crime", was intended to introduce the idea of personal computers to a reader who might be faced with the hardship of using them at work or at home for the first time. It defined basic computer jargon and assured readers that they could master the machine when it inevitably arrived. In his words, being able to program a computer is liberation; "In my experience, you assert control over a computer—show it who's the boss—by making it do something unique. That means programming it....If you devote a couple of hours to programming a new machine, you'll feel better about it ever afterwards". In the book, Crichton predicts a number of events in the history of computer development, that computer networks would increase in importance as a matter of convenience, including the sharing of information and pictures that we see on-line today which the telephone never could. He also makes predictions for computer games, dismissing them as "the hula hoops of the '80s", and saying "already there are indications that the mania for twitch games may be fading. " In a section of the book called "Microprocessors, or how I flunked biostatistics at Harvard," Crichton again seeks his revenge on the medical school teacher who had given him abnormally low grades in college. Within the book, Crichton included many self-written demonstrative Applesoft (for Apple II) and BASICA (for IBM PC compatibles) programs.

Then, in 1988, he published *Travels*, which also contains autobiographical episodes covered in a similar fashion to his 1970 book *Five Patients*.

Literary techniques

Crichton's novels, including *Jurassic Park*, have been described by *The Guardian* as "harking back to the fantasy adventure fiction of Sir Arthur Conan Doyle, Jules Verne, Edgar Rice Burroughs, and Edgar Wallace, but with a contemporary spin, assisted by cutting-edge technology references made accessible for the general reader". According to *The Guardian*, "Michael Crichton wasn't really interested in characters, but his innate talent for storytelling enabled him to breathe new life into the science fiction thriller". Like *The Guardian*, *The New York Times* has also noted the boys' adventure quality to his novels interfused with modern technology and science. According to *The New York Times*,
All the Crichton books depend to a certain extent on a little frisson of fear and suspense: that's what kept you turning the pages. But a deeper source of their appeal was the author's extravagant care in working out the clockwork mechanics of his experiments — the DNA replication in *Jurassic Park,* the time travel in *Timeline,* the submarine technology in *Sphere.* The novels have embedded in them little lectures or mini-seminars on, say, the Bernoulli principle, voice-recognition software or medieval jousting etiquette ... The best of the Crichton novels have about them a boys' adventure quality. They owe something to the Saturday-afternoon movie serials that Mr. Crichton watched as a boy and to the adventure novels of Arthur Conan Doyle (from whom Mr. Crichton borrowed the title *The Lost World* and whose example showed that a novel could never have too many dinosaurs). These books thrive on yarn spinning, but they also take immense delight in the inner workings of things (as opposed to people, women especially), and they make the world — or the made-up world, anyway — seem boundlessly interesting. Readers come away entertained and also with the belief, not entirely illusory, that they have actually learned something"
— *The New York Times* on the works of Michael Crichton
Crichton's works were frequently cautionary; his plots often portrayed scientific advancements going awry, commonly resulting in worst-case scenarios. A notable recurring theme in Crichton's plots is the pathological failure of complex systems and their safeguards, whether biological (*Jurassic Park*), military/organizational (*The Andromeda Strain*), technical (*Airframe*) or cybernetic (*Westworld*). This theme of the inevitable breakdown of "perfect" systems and the failure of "fail-safe measures" can be seen strongly in the poster for *Westworld* (slogan: "*Where nothing*

can possibly go worng ..." (sic)) and in the discussion of chaos theory in *Jurassic Park*.

The use of author surrogate was a feature of Crichton's writings from the beginning of his career. In *A Case of Need*, one of his pseudonymous whodunit stories, Crichton used first-person narrative to portray the hero, a Bostonian pathologist, who is running against the clock to clear a friend's name from medical malpractice in a girl's death from a hack-job abortion.

Some of Crichton's fiction used a literary technique called false document. For example, *Eaters of the Dead* is a fabricated recreation of the Old English epic *Beowulf* in the form of a scholarly translation of Ahmad ibn Fadlan's 10th century manuscript. Other novels, such as *The Andromeda Strain* and *Jurassic Park*, incorporated fictionalized scientific documents in the form of diagrams, computer output, DNA sequences, footnotes and bibliography. Some of his novels included authentic published scientific works to illustrate his point, such as in *The Terminal Man* and *State of Fear*.

Crichton sometimes used a premise in which a diverse group of "experts" or specialists are assembled to tackle a unique problem requiring their individual talents and knowledge. This was done in "Andromeda Strain" as well as "Sphere," "Jurassic Park," and to a far lesser extent "Timeline." Sometimes the individual characters in this dynamic work in the private sector and are suddenly called upon by the government to form an immediate response team once some incident or discovery triggers their mobilization. This premise or plot device has been imitated and used by other authors and screenwriters in several books, movies and television shows since.

At the prose level, one of Crichton's trademarks was the single word paragraph: a dramatic question answered by a single word on its own as a paragraph.

Works

Novels

Year	Title	Notes
1966	Odds On	as John Lange
1967	Scratch One	as John Lange
1968	Easy Go	as John Lange (also titled as *The Last Tomb*)
	A Case of Need	as Jeffery Hudson (re-released as Crichton in 1993)
1969	Zero Cool	as John Lange
	The Andromeda Strain	
	The Venom Business	as John Lange
1970	Drug of Choice	as John Lange (also titled Overkill)
	Dealing	as Michael Douglas (with brother Douglas Crichton)
	Grave Descend	as John Lange
1972	Binary	as John Lange (re-released as Crichton in 1993)
	The Terminal Man	
1975	The Great Train Robbery	
1976	Eaters of the Dead	
1980	Congo	
1987	Sphere	
1990	Jurassic Park	
1992	Rising Sun	
1994	Disclosure	
1995	The Lost World	
1996	Airframe	
1999	Timeline	
2002	Prey	
2004	State of Fear	
2006	Next	
2009	Pirate Latitudes	posthumous publication
2011	Micro	posthumous publication (unfinished)

Short stories

Year	Title	Originally published	Not
1957	"Johnny at 8:30"	*First Words* (1993)	poe
1960	"[Untitled]"	*First Words* (1993)	
1961	"Life Goes to a Party"	*First Words* (1993)	
1961	"The Most Important Part of the Lab"	*First Words* (1993)	
1968	"Villa of Assassins"	*Stag Annual* (1968)	as J Lan exc fron Scr On (19
1968	"How Does That Make You Feel?"	*Playboy* (November 1968)	as J Huc
1970	"The Death Divers"	*Man's World* (December 1970)	as J Lan exc fron Gra Des (19
1971	"The Most Powerful Tailor in the World"	*Playboy* (September 1971)	
1984	"Mousetrap: A Tale of Computer Crime"	*Life* (January 1984)	
2003	"Blood Doesn't Come Out"	*McSwenney's Mammoth Treasury of Thrilling Tales* (2003)	

Non-fiction

Year	Title
1970	*Five Patients*
1977	*Jasper Johns*
1983	*Electronic Life*
1988	*Travels*

As a film director and screenwriter

Crichton wrote or directed several motion pictures and episodes of TV series. In the 1970s in particular he was intent on being a successful filmmaker. Crichton wrote several episodes for the television series *Insight* in the early 1970s. His first film, *Pursuit* (1972), was a TV movie both written and directed by Crichton that is based on his novel *Binary*.

Westworld was the first feature film that used 2D computer-generated imagery (CGI).

Crichton directed the film *Coma*, adapted from a Robin Cook novel. There are other similarities in terms of genre and the fact that both Cook and Crichton had medical degrees, were of similar age, and wrote about similar subjects.

Other major releases directed by Crichton include *The Great Train Robbery* (1979), *Looker* (1981), *Runaway* (1984), and *Physical Evidence* (1989). The middle two films were science fiction, set in the very near future at the time, and included particularly flashy styles of filmmaking, for their time.

He wrote the screenplay for the movies *Extreme Close Up* (1973) and *Twister* (1996), the latter co-written with Anne-Marie Martin, his wife at the time. While *Jurassic Park* and *The Lost World* were both based on Crichton's novels, *Jurassic Park III* was not (though scenes from the *Jurassic Park* novel were incorporated into the third film, such as the aviary).

Crichton was also the creator and executive producer of the television drama *ER*. He had written what became the pilot script in 1974. Twenty years later Steven Spielberg helped develop the show, serving as a producer on season one and offering advice (he insisted on Julianna Margulies becoming a regular, for example). It was also through Spielberg's Amblin Entertainment that John Wells was contacted to be the show's executive producer. In 1994, Crichton achieved the unique distinction of having a No. 1 movie, *Jurassic Park*, a No. 1 TV show, *ER*, and a No. 1 book, *Disclosure*.

Crichton wrote only three episodes of *ER*:
Episode 1–1: "24 Hours"
Episode 1–2: "Day One"
Episode 1–3: "Going Home"

Computer games

Amazon is a graphical text adventure game created by Michael Crichton and produced by John Wells under Trillium Corp. *Amazon* was released in the United States in 1984, and it runs on Apple II, Atari 8-bit, Atari ST, Commodore 64, and the DOS systems. It sold more than 100,000 copies, making it a significant commercial success at the time. It featured plot elements similar to those later used in *Congo*.

In 1999, Crichton founded Timeline Computer Entertainment with David Smith. Despite signing a multi-title publishing deal with Eidos Interactive, only one game was ever published, *Timeline*. Released on December 8, 2000, for the PC, the game received negative reviews and sold poorly.

Speeches

Crichton delivered a number of notable speeches in his lifetime.

Intelligence Squared "Global Warming is Not a Crisis" debate

On March 14, 2007, Intelligence Squared held a debate in New York City entitled *Global Warming is Not a Crisis*, moderated by Brian Lehrer. Crichton was on the *for the motion* side along with Richard Lindzen and Philip Stott against Gavin Schmidt, Richard Somerville, and Brenda Ekwurzel. Before the debate, the audience were largely on the *Against the motion* side at 57% vs 30% in favor of the *for* side, with a 12% undecided. At the end of the debate, there was a notable shift in the audience vote at 46% vs 42% in favor of the *for the motion side* leaving the debate with the conclusion that Crichton's group won. Schmidt later described the debate in a RealClimate blog posting, "Crichton went with the crowd-pleasing condemnation of private jet-flying liberals – very popular, even among the private jet-flying Eastsiders present) and the apparent hypocrisy of people who think that global warming is a problem using any energy at all." Those for the motion had presented the agreed scientific consensus of IPCC reports, the audience was "apparently more convinced by the entertaining narratives from Crichton and Stott (not so sure about Lindzen) than they were by our drier fare. Entertainment-wise it's hard to blame them. Crichton is extremely polished and Stott has a touch of the revivalist preacher about him. Comparatively, we were pretty dull."

In the debate, although he admitted that man must have at some point contributed to global warming but not necessarily caused it, Crichton argued that most of the media and attention of the general public are being dedicated to the uncertain anthropogenic global warming scares instead of the more urgent issues like poverty. He also suggested that private jets be banned as they add more carbon dioxide in the atmosphere for the benefit of the few who could afford them.

The scientific consensus is that the Earth's climate system is unequivocally warming, and it is more than 90% certain that humans are causing it through activities that increase concentrations of greenhouse gases in the atmosphere, such as deforestation and burning fossil fuels. Scientific consensus holds that on balance the impacts of global warming will be significantly negative, especially with relatively large amounts of warming.

Genetic research and legislative needs

While writing *Next*, Crichton concluded that laws covering genetic research desperately needed to be revised, and spoke to Congressional staff members about problems ahead. A Talk to Legislative Staffers Washington, D.C. September 14, 2006

Complexity theory and environmental management

In previous speeches, Crichton criticized environmental groups for failing to incorporate complexity theory. Here he explains in detail why complexity theory is essential to environmental management, using the history of Yellowstone Park as an example of what not to do. Washington Center for Complexity and Public Policy Washington, D.C. November 6, 2005

Testimony before the United States Senate

Together with climate scientists, Crichton was invited to testify before the Senate in September 2005, as an expert witness on global warming. Committee on Environment and Public Works Washington, D.C.

Caltech Michelin Lecture

"Aliens Cause Global Warming" January 17, 2003. In the spirit of his science fiction writing Crichton details the fallacy of Carl Sagan's nuclear winter and SETI Drake equations relative to global warming alarmism.

The Case for Skepticism on Global Warming

On January 25, 2005 at the National Press Club Washington, D.C., Crichton delivered a detailed explanation of why he criticized the consensus view on global warming. Using published UN data, he argued that claims for catastrophic warming arouse doubt; that reducing CO is vastly more difficult than what is commonly presumed; and why societies are morally unjustified in spending vast sums on a speculative issue when people around the world are dying of starvation and disease.

Science Policy in the 21st century

Crichton outlined several issues before a joint meeting of liberal and conservative think tanks. Joint Session AEI-Brookings Institution Washington, D.C. January 25, 2005

Environmentalism as Religion

This was not the first discussion of environmentalism as a religion, but it caught on and was widely quoted. Crichton explains his view that religious approaches to the environment are inappropriate and cause damage to the natural world they intend to protect. Commonwealth Club San Francisco, California September 15, 2003

Ritual Abuse, Hot Air, and Missed Opportunities: Science Views Media

The AAAS invited Crichton to address scientists' concerns about how they are portrayed in the media. American Association for the Advancement of Science Anaheim, California January 25, 1999

Mediasaurus: The Decline of Conventional Media

A 1993 speech which predicted the decline of mainstream media. National Press Club, Washington, D.C. April 7, 1993.

Reception

Criticism of Crichton's environmental views

Many of Crichton's publicly expressed views, particularly on subjects like the global warming controversy, have been contested by a number of scientists and commentators. An example is meteorologist Jeffrey Masters' review of *State of Fear*:

Flawed or misleading presentations of global warming science exist in the book, including those on Arctic sea ice thinning, correction of land-based temperature measurements for the urban heat island effect, and satellite vs. ground-based measurements of Earth's warming. I will spare the reader additional details. On the positive side, Crichton does emphasize the little-appreciated fact that while most of the world has been warming the past few decades, most of Antarctica has seen a cooling trend. The Antarctic ice sheet is actually expected to increase in mass over the next 100 years due to increased precipitation, according to the IPCC."

Peter Doran, author of the paper in the January 2002, issue of *Nature* which reported the finding referred to above that some areas of Antarctica had cooled between 1986 and 2000, wrote an opinion piece in the July 27, 2006, *The New York Times* in which he stated "Our results have been misused as 'evidence' against global warming by Michael Crichton in his novel *State of Fear*." Al Gore said on March 21, 2007, before a U.S. House committee: "The planet has a fever. If your baby has a fever, you go to the doctor [...] if your doctor tells you you need to intervene here, you don't say 'Well, I read a science fiction novel that tells me it's not a problem'." This has been recognized by several commentators as a reference to *State of Fear*.

Michael Crowley

In his 2006 novel, *Next*, Crichton introduced a character named "Mick Crowley" who is a Yale graduate and a Washington D.C.-based political columnist. "Crowley" was portrayed by Crichton as a child molester with a small penis. From page 227 as quoted in *The New York Times*: "Alex Burnet was in the middle of the most difficult trial of her career, a rape case involving the sexual assault of a two-year-old boy in Malibu. The defendant, thirty-year-old Mick Crowley, was a Washington-based political columnist who was visiting his sister-in-law when he experienced an overwhelming urge to have anal sex with her young son, still in diapers." The character is a minor one who does not appear elsewhere in the book.

A real person named Michael Crowley is also a Yale graduate, and a senior editor of *The New Republic*, a liberal Washington D.C.-based political magazine. In March 2006, the real Crowley had written an article strongly critical of Crichton for his stance on global warming in *State of Fear*. Crowley responded by proposing "a corollary to the small penis rule. Call it the small man rule: If someone offers substantive criticism of an author, and the author responds by hitting below the belt, as it were, then he's conceding that the critic has won."

Awards

Mystery Writers of America's Edgar Allan Poe Award, Best Novel, 1969 — *A Case of Need*

Association of American Medical Writers Award, 1970

Mystery Writers of America's Edgar Allan Poe Award, Best Motion Picture, 1980 — *The Great Train Robbery*

Named to the list of the "Fifty Most Beautiful People" by *People* magazine, 1992

Academy of Motion Picture Arts and

Sciences Technical Achievement Award, 1994
Writers Guild of America Award, Best Long Form Television Script of 1995
George Foster Peabody Award, 1994 — *ER*
Primetime Emmy Award for Outstanding Drama Series, 1996 — *ER*
Ankylosaur named *Crichtonsaurus bohlini*, 2002
The American Association of Petroleum Geologists Journalism Award, 2006

Associations

Phi Beta Kappa
Author's Guild
Writers Guild of America
P.E.N. America Center
Directors Guild of America
Academy of Television Arts and Sciences
Member of Academy of Motion Picture Arts and Sciences
Board of Directors, International Design Conference at Aspen, 1985–91
Board of Trustees, Western Behavioral Sciences Institute, La Jolla, 1986–91
Board of Overseers, Harvard University, 1990–96
Board of Directors, Drug Strategies, 1994–2008
Author's Guild Council, 1995–2008
Board of Directors, Gorilla Foundation, 2002–2008
Board of Trustees, Los Angeles County Museum of Art, 2006–2008

Personal life

Crichton believed in God.

As an adolescent Crichton felt isolated because of his height (at 6'9"). As an adult he was acutely aware of his intellect, which often left him feeling alienated from the people around him. During the 1970s and 1980s he consulted psychics and enlightenment gurus to make him feel more socially acceptable and to improve his karma. As a result of these experiences, Crichton practiced meditation throughout much of his life.

Crichton was a workaholic. When drafting a novel, which would typically take him six or seven weeks, Crichton withdrew completely to follow what he called "a structured approach" of ritualistic self-denial. As he neared writing the end of each book, he would rise increasingly early each day, meaning that he would sleep for less than four hours by going to bed at 10 pm and waking at 2 am. In 1992, Crichton was ranked among *People* magazine's 50 most beautiful people.

Marriages and children

He married five times; four of the marriages ended in divorce. He was married to Suzanna Childs, Joan Radam (1965–1970), Kathleen St. Johns (1978–1980), and actress Anne-Marie Martin (1987–2003), the mother of his daughter Taylor Anne (born 1989). At the time of his death, Crichton was married to Sherri Alexander, who was six months pregnant with their son. John Michael Todd Crichton was born on February 12, 2009.

Intellectual property cases

In November 2006, at the National Press Club in Washington, D.C., Crichton joked that he considered himself an expert in intellectual property law. He had been involved in several lawsuits with others claiming credit for his work. In 1985, the Ninth Circuit Court of Appeals heard *Berkic v. Crichton*, 761 F.2d 1289 (1985). Plaintiff Ted Berkic wrote a screenplay called *Reincarnation Inc.*, which he claims Crichton plagiarized for the movie *Coma*. The court ruled in Crichton's favor, stating the works were not substantially similar. In the 1996 case, *Williams v. Crichton*, 84 F.3d 581 (2d Cir. 1996), Geoffrey Williams claimed that *Jurassic Park* violated his copyright covering his dinosaur-themed children's stories published in the late 1980s. The court granted summary judgment in favor of Crichton. In 1998, A United States District Court in Missouri heard the case of *Kessler v. Crichton* that actually went all the way to a jury trial, unlike the other cases. Plaintiff Stephen Kessler claimed the movie *Twister* was based on his work *Catch the Wind*. It took the jury about 45 minutes to reach a verdict in favor of Crichton. After the verdict, Crichton refused to shake Kessler's hand. At the National Press Club in 2006, Crichton summarized his intellectual property legal problems by stating, "I always win."

Illness and death

In accordance with the private way in which Crichton lived his life, his throat cancer was not made public until his death. According to Crichton's brother Douglas, Crichton was diagnosed with lymphoma in early 2008. He was undergoing chemotherapy treatment at the time of his death, and Crichton's physicians and family members had been expecting him to make a recovery. He unexpectedly died of the disease on November 4, 2008, at the age of 66.

Michael's talent outscaled even his own dinosaurs of *Jurassic Park*. He was the greatest at blending science with big theatrical concepts, which is what gave credibility to dinosaurs again walking the earth. In the early days, Michael had just sold *The Andromeda Strain* to Robert Wise at Universal and I had recently signed on as a contract TV director there. My first assignment was to show Michael Crichton around the Universal lot. We became friends and professionally *Jurassic Park*, *ER*, and *Twister* followed. Michael was a gentle soul who reserved his flamboyant side for his novels. There is no one in the wings that will ever take his place.

—Steven Spielberg on Michael Crichton's death.

Crichton had an extensive collection of 20th century American art, which was auctioned by Christie's in May 2010.

Unfinished novels

On April 6, 2009, Crichton's publisher, HarperCollins, announced the posthumous publication of two of his novels. The first was *Pirate Latitudes*, found completed on his computer by his assistant after he died. This was the second of a two-novel deal that started with *Next*.

The other novel, titled *Micro*, is a techno-thriller that was released in November 2011. The novel explores the outer edges of new science and technology. The novel is based on Michael Crichton's notes and files, and was roughly a third of the way finished when he died. HarperCollins publisher Jonathan Burnham, and Crichton's agent Lynn Nesbit, looked for a co-writer to finish the novel. Ultimately, Richard Preston was chosen to complete the book.

Film and television

Novels adapted into films

Year	Title	Filmmaker/Director
1971	The Andromeda Strain	Robert Wise
1972	Dealing: Or the Berkeley-to-Boston Forty-Brick Lost-Bag Blues	Paul Williams
1972	The Carey Treatment (A Case of Need)	Blake Edwards
1974	The Terminal Man	Mike Hodges
1979	The First Great Train Robbery	Michael Crichton
1993	Jurassic Park	Steven Spielberg
1993	Rising Sun	Philip Kaufman
1994	Disclosure	Barry Levinson
1995	Congo	Frank Marshall
1997	The Lost World: Jurassic Park	Steven Spielberg
1998	Sphere	Barry Levinson
1999	The 13th Warrior (Eaters of the Dead)	John McTiernan
2003	Timeline	Richard Donner
2008	The Andromeda Strain (TV miniseries)	Mikael Salomon

As a screenwriter and/or director

Year	Title	Notes
1972	Pursuit (TV film)	Co-Writer/Director
1973	Westworld	Writer/Director
1978	Coma	Writer/Director
1979	The First Great Train Robbery	Writer/Director
1981	Looker	Writer/Director
1984	Runaway	Writer/Director
1989	Physical Evidence	Director
1993	Jurassic Park	Co-Writer
1993	Rising Sun	Co-Writer
1996	Twister	Co-Writer/Producer

TV series

Year	Title	Notes
1980	Beyond Westworld	Creator/Writer
1994–2009	ER	Creator/Writer/Executive Producer

Source http://en.wikipedia.org/wiki/Michael_Crichton

Saul Mariaschin

No. 4
Guard
Personal information
Born September 1, 1924
Nationality American
Died 1991 (aged 66–67)
Listed height 5 ft 11 in (1.80 m)
Listed weight 165 lb (75 kg)
Career information
College Harvard
Career history
1947–1948 Boston Celtics
Stats at Basketball-Reference.com
Saul Mariaschin (September 1, 1924 – 1991) was an American professional basketball player who competed in the Basketball Association of America during the 1947–48 season. He played college basketball at Harvard, and in the BAA played for the Boston Celtics.

Source http://en.wikipedia.org/wiki/Saul_Mariaschin

Tony Lupien

Tony Lupien
First baseman
Born: April 23, 1917
Chelmsford, Massachusetts
Died: July 9, 2004 (aged 87)
Norwich, Vermont
Batted: Left   **Threw:** Left
MLB debut
September 12, 1940 for the Boston Red Sox
Last MLB appearance
October 3, 1948 for the Chicago White Sox
Career statistics
Batting average .268
Home runs 18
Runs batted in 230
Teams
Boston Red Sox (1940, 1942–1943)
Philadelphia Phillies (1944–1945)
Chicago White Sox (1948)

Ulysses John "Tony" Lupien (April 23, 1917 – July 9, 2004) was an American first baseman in Major League Baseball. He was a left-handed batter who played for the Boston Red Sox, Philadelphia Phillies and Chicago White Sox. Lupien was an all-around athlete and successful coach.

Early life

Lupien was born in Chelmsford, Massachusetts, the son of Eugenie (née Gosselin) and Ulysses J. Lupien. His parents were of French Canadian descent, and he was named "Ulysses" because of his great-grandfather's admiration for president Ulysses S. Grant. He graduated from Harvard University in 1939. At Harvard, he was captain of the baseball team as a junior and of the basketball team as a senior. He was the Eastern Intercollegiate League batting champion in 1938 and 1939, and he also was a quarterback for his freshman football team.

Career

Upon graduation from Harvard, Lupien signed a professional baseball contract with the Red Sox and played the 1939 season for the Double-A Scranton Red Sox Eastern League championship team. He made his major league debut for the Red Sox on September 12, 1940. One of his most productive seasons came in 1942 when he batted .281 with three home runs and 70 runs batted in for the Red Sox. He was traded to the Phillies where he played in 1944 and early in 1945, before serving in the U.S. Navy during World War II. In the 1944 season he hit .283 with five homers, 52 RBI, 82 runs, 23 doubles, 9 triples and 18 stolen bases. In 1948, he played for the White Sox.

Lupien finished his MLB career hitting .268 with 18 home runs, 230 RBI, 285 runs, 92 doubles, 30 triples, and 57 stolen bases in 614 games. In 1949, he played with Triple-A Toledo (American Association). He concluded his professional career from 1951–53 and in 1955 when he was a player as well as field and general manager with the Jamestown Falcons and Corning Independents, in the PONY League. From 1951 to 1956, he was head basketball coach at Middlebury College, compiling a record of 60–49 in five seasons.

In 1956, Lupien was hired as Dartmouth College's baseball coach. He spent 21 seasons at the school and guided his teams to 313 wins, 305 losses and three ties, winning the Eastern Intercollegiate League championship four times (1963, 1967, 1969–70). His 1970 team advanced to the College World Series at Omaha, Nebraska where it finished fifth. That team had a 24–10 record that included a 21-game win streak. He was also the Dartmouth freshman basketball coach from 1956 to 1968.

Personal life and legacy

Lupien retired from coaching in 1977, but continued to work for many years as a stockbroker with various firms in New England. He died in Norwich, Vermont, at 87 years of age. He was married to Natalie Nichols, and later to Mildred Robinson. His grandson is wrestler and actor John Cena.

Lupien was recognized for decades as a great teacher and mentor. He was also an outspoken observer of labor relations in professional baseball. In 1980 he collaborated with writer Lee Lowenfish to author *The Imperfect Diamond*, a book that remains a definitive text on baseball labor from the introduction of the reserve clause in 1879 to the litigation in the 1970s that led to free agency.

Source http://en.wikipedia.org/wiki/Tony_Lupien

Wyndol Gray

No. 4, 3
Guard/Forward
Personal information
Born   March 30, 1922
Died   March 20, 1994 (aged 71)
High school   Akron South Akron, Ohio
Listed height   6 ft 1 in (1.85 m)
Listed weight   175 lb (79 kg)
Career information
College   Bowling Green Harvard
Pro career   1946–1948
Career history
Boston Celtics (1946–47) [BAA]
Providence Steamrollers (1947–48) [BAA]
St. Louis Bombers (1947–48) [BAA]
Career highlights and awards
1945 Consensus First Team All-American (NCAA)
1946 Second Team All-American (The Sporting News)
Bowling Green Athletics Hall of Fame (1964)
Career BAA statistics
Points   363
Rebounds   Not tracked
Assists   50
Stats at Basketball-Reference.com

Wyndol Woodrow Gray (March 30, 1922 – March 20, 1994) was an American professional basketball player in the 1940s.

Gray played at Akron South High School in Akron, Ohio and went on to play collegiately at Bowling Green State University in 1942. At the time, freshmen were allowed to play to compensate for a shortage of college-age players due to World War II. Gray played on future Hall of Fame coach Harold Anderson's first team at Bowling Green. He led the team in scoring at 22.3 points per game and the Falcons went 18–4.

Gray joined the Navy after the season, and returned to Bowling Green for the 1944–45 season as a part of the V-12 Navy College Training Program and, along with big man Don Otten, led the Falcons to the final of the 1945 National Invitation Tournament, where they were defeated by the George Mikan-led DePaul Blue Demons. After the season, Gray was named a consensus first team All-American – Bowling Green's first in basketball.

In 1945–46, Gray played at Harvard. There he led the Crimson to their first NCAA tournament appearance and at the conclusion of the season he was named a second team All-American by the *Sporting News* magazine, giving him the unusual distinction of being named an All-American at two different universities.

After his college career was over, Gray played for Honey Russell on the first Boston Celtics team in 1946–47. He played in 55 of the team's 60 games and finished third on the team in scoring at 6.4 points per game. The following season, the Celtics traded Gray to the St. Louis Bombers for guard Cecil Hankins. Eleven games into his Bombers career, Gray was again traded, this time to the Providence Steamrollers for forward Ariel Maughan. Gray's Steamrollers career lasted only one game.

Wyndol Gray died on March 20, 1994.

Source http://en.wikipedia.org/wiki/Wyndol_Gray